Execute Like a Pro

A Gameplan for Success

By Bill Shreffler and Jackie Smith

With Phil Seibert and Dee Porter

Cover photograph courtesy of Calico Days Photography

My first exposure to Bill's football theme was the Michigan Blizzard Football kick off meeting. It was electrifying and energizing and Bill had a completely different way to look at building a team. It didn't take years to pull it all together and develop a well-oiled machine. That was accomplished within a couple of months and then business really took off.

Jim Holanda, CEO – RCN/Choice Cable

The Michigan Blizzard was a huge success that exceeded all expectations. I find several of Bill's former team mates working for us and still carrying on the same management philosophy and programs. What Bill did with the Blizzard and Cyclone teams was not just short term success, but he instilled in his people a strong propensity for extraordinary achievement. Bill has a legacy of coaching great managers that have gone on to create their own teams and the cycle keeps repeating itself over and over.

Dave Barford, past Charter Communication's COO and Senior Vice President of Charter Communication's Western Division

The whole thing is you have to have a passion for something; also, dedication, responsibility and discipline.

Bob DeMarco, past Center, St. Louis Cardinals, Dolphins, Browns and Rams

What Bill does is a real art. Bill's KPI approach takes the mystery out of it, and brought the numbers to life. The way Bill has perfected it, he's put a fun program around it, theme based, sport based program which gets people to interact. It works really well, particularly on geographically dispersed organizations.

Mike Wylie, past Suddenlink CAO, CFO Broadstripe and current CFO Pulse Broadband

It took the first 6 months of 2000 to get everybody's sea legs and pulling in the same direction. But once we did, sales and profitability took off like a hockey stick - it went straight up. Let me say again, everybody was pulling in the same direction and for the same goal.

Terie Hannay, past Regional Director, Customer Care, Charter Communications, Michigan

What I will proudly say is that by following Bill's approach, I know I accomplished more in those two years than I ever thought I could. And that continues to this day…

Jim Holanda, CEO – RCN/Choice Cable

Again, responsibility, discipline and passion for something are what you basically carry over from football into a business.

Bob DeMarco, past Center, St. Louis Cardinals, Dolphins, Browns and Rams

At the yearend celebration the entire organization was there. We didn't have some dry corporate dinner with a band later – but a huge blowout! Yes, it was incredibly fun. Everyone knew what they were celebrating and why they were there. It was truly something special for the entire regional team - and I still have my ring!

Terie Hannay, past Regional Director, Customer Care, Charter Communications, Michigan

ACKNOWLEDGEMENTS

I have always known that I am blessed on so many levels. My wonderful wife Kristie has always supported me and encouraged my creativity in my home life and my business ventures. I am also blessed with two beautiful daughters, Jennifer and Lauren, and their families. They have brought me much happiness over the years. I have also learned many things from my son, Sam. Never, ever quit. No matter how hard things may get. He is a living testament to perseverance. I also want to thank all of the terrific team mates I have worked with over the years. You all have provided me with incredible blessings and friendship. I hope this book helps new and current leaders achieve great levels of business and personal success in the future.

Bill Shreffler

Rarely do we accomplish anything noteworthy completely on our own. As a rookie in 1963 with very limited football experience, the Cardinal receiver coach Fran Polsfoot saw something that I or no one else did. Consequently he insisted I not be cut and given time to mature as a player. Thank you Coach.
Football life demands a lot from the families of players. Had it not been for my wife Geri's support and understanding, which remains today, my career would have ended early. It is to her credit we have 4 exceptional children who have produced 14 wonderful grandchildren, providing a sea of hugs and kisses!

Jackie Smith

TABLE OF CONTENTS

Preface

Chapter 1   How It All Started

Chapter 2   Building the Team

Chapter 3   Building Your Plan and KPIs

Chapter 4   The Kick Off, Go Live With Your Plan

Chapter 5   First Possession, Game Films and Initial Observations In Real Time

Chapter 6   Expanding the Plan, Executing the Plan and Making It Work...HALFTIME!

Chapter 7   Because He Said To – He's The Coach... Staying Focused

Chapter 8   Halftime and the Transition into the Third Quarter

Chapter 9   Third Quarter – It Starts Again, the Concept of Hustle...

Chapter 10   Third Quarter – Climbing The Mountain

Chapter 11   Fourth Quarter – Executing, Red Zone, Third-Down Conversions, KPIs and Bringing It All Home"

Chapter 12   The Final Drive Begins

Chapter 13   Celebrating Success

PREFACE

This book is the culmination of all of the fun I've had running organizations over the past 30 years. I learned a lot of hard lessons and saw some things along the way that I knew would not work. I also discovered that there is a secret to success in business. It may not be something you learn in business school either. Just about anyone can be a good tactician but it takes a special person to be a great leader. I believe that leadership skills can be taught, but you need the right foundation and the right belief system for your skills to flourish. So this book is focused toward helping anyone who wants to be a better leader and help that leader achieve great success. It doesn't matter if you are a supervisor or a CEO, these tips will help you succeed. Specifically, you need to:

- Have integrity in everything you do. No question.
- Care about your customer. Without this you have nothing. Job number 1.
- Care about what you are doing. Believe in your company, your plan and where you want to go in your life.
- Care about your team. I mean really care. Don't just *tolerate* your team mates. Get to know them and their families. Know their spouses name and their kids' names. Start a Monday discussion with 'how was your weekend' and mean it. Care about what they tell you. If you try to act like you care but really don't, they will know and they will not trust you.
- Bring fun into work. It's OK to laugh and enjoy the time you have to be away from your family. You have to be there no matter what - so have fun! Life is too short.
- Celebrate your success and enjoy the fruits of your labor. I don't mean bring in donuts, I mean **really** celebrate!

It is my intention to help you learn or grow your skills in these areas. I have worked in both the manufacturing and service industries in my career. I have run organizations that produced over $1 billion in revenue annually. I have been an entrepreneur several times as well. The skills I listed above have always helped my team beat our goals. I also want to share the Mission Statement I have used for over 24 years:

- Take care of the customer
- Take care of each other
- Do what you say you are going to do
- Celebrate your successes in a meaningful way

Do you notice how the Mission Statement coincides exactly to the skills I listed earlier? This is not by accident.

Before we get into the book, let me introduce some key players that made this book possible.

First there is Jackie Smith. A Hall of Fame Tight End from the St Louis Football Cardinals and a great guy. Jackie and I have become great friends over the past 6 years and we have worked together to bring about some of the successes I detail in the book. Jackie worked closely with me and my team at Broadstripe and at Pulse Broadband. The team loves his 'down home' demeanor but everyone also quickly sees the intelligence he brings to every situation. Jackie has built and been a part of many businesses over his career. He also achieved the pinnacle of any football player's dream when he was inducted into the Football Hall of Fame in 1994. We could not have written this book without his encouragement or his help.

Next I would like to introduce Phil Seibert. Phil and I met in early 2005 when we started a company called Home Boulevard together. We became fast friends and stayed close over the past 7 years. Phil brings terrific business insight to this book. He spent countless hours with Jackie and me asking a ton of probing questions to get to the 'heart of the matter'....'the secret sauce'...the things that really move a business. Phil wrote the words on the page and Jackie and I made sure it caught the essence of what we were trying to bring to you, the reader. In my opinion Phil did a terrific job and I am very thankful for his friendship and his perseverance.

Finally, the "glue" of the group is Dee Porter. She is loved by everyone who works with her. I had the pleasure of meeting her in early 2001 when I came to St Louis with Charter Communications. She was my Executive Assistant initially but eventually she became so much more than that. She keeps everything on an even keel and cares about everyone on the team. Dee has a great sense of humor and she is tireless in making sure that everyone on the team understands what I want to achieve. She has always been the "unofficial" spokesperson for me and Dee always keeps me informed if the team has questions or concerns. This is why Dee and I have stayed together through six different jobs/companies over the past 11 years. I couldn't do this book without her. I am thankful to be a part of her family and have her as a member of my family.

So there is the back-story. Time to dive in. Let's start with a fateful meeting……..

Man, I can't believe I'm sitting here waiting for the CEO of the company to come in to a budget review meeting where I am completely unprepared! I don't know how I can create a budget for a region that does not currently exist. I just met a few of the new Michigan team members recently and I don't know much about their current operations or how they operated in the past. In short I feel like "dead man walking". I hope that the CEO takes pity on me and realizes the situation I am in.

I was originally going to follow the other new region in the budget review but they claimed they weren't ready to go yet so I was put ahead in the queue. To be honest I think the other region's team are as scared as I am so they chickened out and figured I would take the heat in the first meeting making their meeting a little easier. To make matters worse one of the new team members I just met in Michigan called me on my way to St. Louis to tell me he wasn't going to come with me and he wasn't going to stick around and be a part of the new region. So he chickened out too!

Not only do I have to present to the CEO but I have to present to my boss, whom I have been working for only 6 weeks and many members of the corporate team. I can't see any way that this meeting is going to go well……….uh oh….here's comes the CEO. The meeting is starting.

CHAPTER ONE

HOW IT ALL STARTED

Earlier in my career when I became a general manager at Continental Cablevision, I found that one key to success was to mix fun with work. I always believed that leaders need to make the office a great place to work so teammates will have great attitudes about their work. I never forgot some of the places I worked earlier in my career and what a struggle it was to go to work let alone try to be creative.

In those earlier days we had many challenging goals too, so I experimented with some fun themes to help us focus on our work while having a good time.

One such theme was "Rock 'n Roll to the 50s" (our goal was to hit 50,000 customers) and another was "Groovin thru the 60s" (the goal here was to exceed 60,000 customers). Using those themes I had an opportunity to see how well incentives play in business. If you can get someone focused on a theme, that theme becomes overarching. In many ways it makes the day-to-day grind kind of go away. People are more focused on the bigger tasks and goals. It also helps them to look forward to whatever opportunity or excitement comes next.

As I went through the next ten to twelve years of my career it became more obvious to me that I always talked about teams, about moving the ball and about scoring. I always used that terminology.

The bottom line is that I'm from Pittsburgh Pennsylvania. I grew up most of my young life and into my early 20s living in the Pittsburgh area, a huge Steelers fan. I still am a huge fan today. I watched the Steelers in the 70s when they won four Super Bowls with Coach Knoll and his theory of whatever it takes and with Terry Bradshaw and the offense always moving the ball. I also loved how well the defense played and how well the entire team gelled. I had that ingrained in my DNA; I love football and I love the Steelers. I thought about business "teams" exactly as that, a team.

During the drive to the airport after that fateful and disastrous meeting in St. Louis, where I had to present to the Charter CEO, something just clicked. The concept of putting a football team in place for my Michigan Region spilled out of my mind and unfolded before my very eyes. During the flight back I sketched out the broad concepts as they came to mind but I still had some lingering doubts.

I've always been a big believer in getting my team on the phone. When I managed the western operations at Century, I would do weekly staff meeting calls. We would talk about what is happening, as well as what is going to happen. That way everyone would be included in the updates. It really created a team environment so everybody knew they could rely on each other. It also kept the team together even though many miles separated us. We had operations in New Mexico, Colorado, Idaho, California, Wyoming and Montana.
But it was in 1988 and 1989 when I was at Continental in Chicago, that I began using a theme approach. Using "Rock 'n Roll to the 50s" and "Groovin' thru the 60s" those two years were possibly the most creative time of my career.

When I stepped into the Continental General Manager's role it turned out to be similar to my Charter experience in Michigan, but at a much reduced level. Continental was my first GM role. Everybody was looking at what I was doing and always reminding me that I had to prove – everyday, that I was going to become a good leader. That is why I created incentives. The incentives got everybody excited and then things really took off.

By 1995 upper management in the organization started to change and it was not quite the same company. Some of those changes affected what we could do as well as our flexibility, freedom and creativity.

I don't think any organization ever kept me from doing what I wanted to do from a creative standpoint. In Chicago we had been blowing our numbers away for seven years; we got into a rhythm where we were being very successful and it was moving like a machine.

It was like a football team but we didn't call it that. We had other incentives and bonuses but we didn't have an overarching theme. More likely, it hit me at that point; the machine was running and I just didn't think about adding in another theme approach. Also, my operation was one of several in Continental's Chicago region and I always found it interesting that many of the employees from the other Chicago operations wanted to work in my cable system. They saw that we were successful and having fun at the same time.

After Continental, I went out to Century Cable in Colorado Springs, CO. At Century we were building a call center and doing different things. It didn't seem like thematic goals and incentives presented the right opportunity at that point in time. In retrospect it would have been a great thing for me to do but I was focused on other things at that time. When I ran the West Coast region for Century, I had different members of my team that were available to assist other team members in other regions. We created an environment where key members of one team would be available to go help other organizations with whatever issues they had. The team concept is not about "me", it's about "us." It's about how we all can get better and stronger. For much of my career the team concept has been a part of my management style.

The same thing occurred when I went to Cablevision in Long Island, NY. Looking back, I think if I would have used thematic teams in those organizations they would have been even better. The organization was very stretched out so some cohesive team strategy would have worked well in bringing people together to achieve their individual and our collective goals.

In 1998 Paul Allen, of Microsoft fame, bought Charter. Paul had a ton of money and when he bought Charter their customer base was about 1.5 million customers. His goal was to create a big cable company. So he put his resources to work and went on probably one the biggest roundups of cable companies in history. The result was that Charter went from 1.5 million customers to over 7 million customers in literally 1½ to 2 years. I think this was unprecedented at that time.

Basically the answer that Jerry Kent, the Charter Communications CEO, gave to Paul Allen was to make St. Louis the new corporate headquarters and put Charter in charge. At one point, Paul Allen was thinking about letting Marcus cable run the new enterprise, but Jerry and the Charter team got Paul Allen to agree that the Charter management team would get the deal done.

It was such a big task that Jerry went to Dave Barford, SVP of the Western Division, and his other senior team and asked if they could get this task done. The answer was if you get us the right people, yes we can do it. Jerry, Dave and the senior management team's mindset was we can do this. We have just grown so much already, so we'll just make it happen.

I started November 1, 1999. I spent my first 3 days at the North Central Region office in Wisconsin meeting with one of my counterparts. That was my indoctrination into Charter.

After those three days, I jumped on the shuttle plane and flew over to Grand Rapids and dove right in. The guy that had run that part of the region for one of the companies that we were acquiring ended up leaving as I was meeting with our first acquisition. It was crazy; there I was trying to put budgets together with no information. It was just unbelievable. It is a case study in and of itself.

I believe I was hired because I had been responsible for larger organizations. At that point I was running part of Long Island for Cablevision, about 450,000 subscribers and I was responsible for telephony, video and data.

Cablevision at the time was the leader as far as products and services and the cable industry had not caught up yet. That was something that was interesting to Charter. More importantly perhaps, was that I ran everything west of the Mississippi River for Century Communications which was 400,000 to 500,000 subscribers from LA up to Montana to New Mexico. So I had the skills, a proven record of hitting the numbers and running big organizations. The tipping point was probably that I had telephony and data experience, which at that point was not yet on Charter's plate.

In December 1999, I was summoned to St. Louis to participate in a 2000 Budget preparation meeting with our CEO, Jerry Kent, of Charter Communications.

I literally had been on board for about 45 days and was the newly-named Regional Vice President for Charter Communications in Michigan. During those first 45 days I was tasked to create a budget for a region that was yet to be created, with no regional management team, just flying by the seat of my pants.

My task was to bring five different acquisitions into one holistic operating group and create a new region. More specifically, I was to take that yet to-be-created region from 0 customers to about 625,000 customers, literally in a matter of months.

So I was down in St. Louis to meet with the CEO, Jerry Kent, my boss, Dave Barford, and members of the corporate staff.

At that meeting we were to go through the budget process and set up for the year 2000. For me it turned out to be a nightmare.

The worst part was I had to come down to St. Louis, sit in front of a Fortune 500 CEO and explain how I was going to hit my numbers - I didn't even know what these numbers were. The meeting went very badly. Jerry kept asking me questions about what are you going to do with this, what channels are you going to launch and, in general, what are you going to do? My answer was "to be determined" because I really had very little idea of about what I was to accomplish.

During those first few weeks I had yet to meet most of the existing team members. I was scrambling to pull together even the most basic information. Outside of my boss and a few people I met in Michigan, the only guy that I did meet from one of our acquisitions turned out to be a flake. Just prior to leaving for this meeting, he bailed on me at the last minute and quit the next day.

At the meeting it was obvious that I did not have a clue about what I was talking about. Quite candidly, I was fearful but it turned out that I wasn't the only one. I later found out that I was one of the few RVP's hired at Charter without Jerry Kent doing an interview. Jerry had a death in the family so he was unavailable. That left my boss, Dave Barford, and some of the other senior team members to make the decision to hire me. So I am sure Dave was thinking, as he took me to the airport, that this could be career suicide for him. If I completely fell apart that could make him look bad.

While still at Charter headquarters I called my wife. Still a little shaky, I told her how badly the meeting had gone. I also said that when I get off the plane that evening in Grand Rapids I was either going to pull up my resume and look for a job or I was going to be 110% committed and prove everyone wrong. I would either leave now or make this thing a huge success.

At that juncture I wasn't sure which one it would be but I was being honest with Kristie.

During the drive Dave asked me what I was going to do to make the region a success and hit our 2000 budget. I think that all my years of experience came home to roost. I looked at him and what popped out of my mouth was...

"I'm going to form a football team..."

I couldn't believe what I just said. Dave looked at me as if I was the Easter Bunny and said, "You are going to do what?" I said I'm going to go back and form a football team and we are going to win the year.

Dave is a good guy and a good friend today but during that drive he just looked at me and basically changed the subject. He probably thought I was delusional and decided not to go further down that path. He most likely thought I might jump out of the car and into traffic.

Dave would later become the Chief Operating Officer at Charter.

Six to seven months later when we were knocking the ball out of the park, I asked Jerry at a regional meeting what he thought of that budget meeting. He smiled at me and said, "Let's just say I was less than impressed..."

Years later at Charter when I was running the Midwest Division, we had 2 million customers spread over 17 states. After Charter I helped Jerry Kent start Suddenlink and then went on to be the CEO of Broadstripe, another cable operator. The thing that pulled everybody together in each of these companies was the football theme; I found a winning formula.

Key Take-Aways from Chapter 1

- Allow yourself to be creative, go ahead and take a chance
- Don't run from a challenge. Dig in and make it happen
- Never lose your sense of humor…never, ever!!

Interview with Team Mates and Partners

> I always had a dream about how I would get into pro football.
>
> I grew up in NJ, went to St. Mary's and in our freshmen year they took us to see the Giants versus Pittsburgh Steelers in 1956. The next year we went again and saw Detroit Lions against the Giants. I always had the idea I wanted to play one day. I went to college in Indiana, got some recognition, transferred to Dayton and was drafted by Chicago Cardinals in 1959, and then graduated in 1961.
>
> The whole thing is you have to have a passion for something; also, dedication, responsibility and discipline.
>
> I learned from my father if you have an 8am appointment you're there at 7:45 am. That always stuck in my mind, and in business it was the same thing.
>
> **Bob DeMarco**
> **Past Center, St. Louis Cardinals, Dolphins, Browns, Rams**

> Obviously we all had a big job ahead of us, but Michigan had no legacy Charter properties to anchor from so Bill had to create a team from many disparate companies. This was a tall order with no time to get to know one another; Bill definitely had the toughest job.
>
> **Dave Barford, past Charter Communication's COO and Senior Vice President of Charter Communication's Western Division**

CHAPTER TWO
BUILDING THE TEAM

It's my belief the concept of using a football theme really reduced the time it took to build a team.

After landing in Michigan and returning home, I said to my wife Kristie we are going to make this challenge into a huge success. We are going to form a football team and make it happen. Kristie knows me well and she knows I can be "a little out there" from time to time so she said "great"!

The next day I walked into my regional office and I didn't have much of a regional team except I hired Rudy Tober as my head of marketing, Gary Massaglia who was head of one of my operating units and my VP of Fiscal Operations, Dave Gilles. I walked in and said hey this is what we need to do, let's figure it out. We got a big white board up and started talking about themes and reached out to my operating heads and asked them to come up with names for teams and got them to be a part of it and we kept it hush-hush.

During the next couple of weeks we finished preparing our gameplan. Then as part of the announcement I said, I want everybody, including all the new management, at this hotel… on this day. They all came and they were scared because each group had been acquired. I'm sure each of them thought "What could this possibly be about?" It could only be bad news.

We brought them into a conference room and sat them down for about 3 – 4 minutes tops. One of my team members was a reporter and was wearing a goofy old reporter's hat. I walked in wearing a football jersey with the numbers '00' on the back and front signifying the year 2000; 'Shreffler' was also on the back of the jersey. I went up to the podium.

As I turned to them with a serious look, I smiled and said, "Good afternoon ladies and gentlemen. I am here to announce that there is a new football franchise in Michigan called the Charter Michigan Blizzard".

My team member, the guy who played the part of the reporter, asked several questions including what are your plans for 2000. Where will you play your games? Who is on your team? I said, "great questions. We held a draft and the following members have been drafted onto the Michigan Blizzard team…"

I started reading the names and when I read someone's name I told them to stand up. We gave them a round of applause and I threw them a jersey with their name on the back in addition to '00' on the front and back. Most of the people sitting in the chairs looked at me and were a bit confused. They came here with the dreaded thought of being fired and now were being thrown a jersey with their name on it?

When we were done with the kickoff I said "I want everybody to put your jerseys on right now and leave them on for the next two days". I told them this process is all about defining the gameplan for the Michigan Blizzard.

- What are our goals?
- Who are we as a team?
- How are we going to go forward?
- How will we specifically beat our goals?

Soon everyone started to get excited – just as soon as they figured out that they weren't getting fired and that this "football thing" was going to be a lot of fun. It was a great thing to watch as their fears and concerns were replaced by excitement. When they arrived they didn't know what was going to happen to them. Now suddenly, it went from bad - to getting a shirt with their name on the back and proving that they were part of the team. It was a complete 180!

That is when we sat down in the meetings. I said, "Look, here is our budget. This budget was put together on basically a shoestring. We have to hit this budget but we have to aim higher than this budget..." We needed to beat our budget by at least 5% to win the year. Big task.

So that is all we talked about. We really dug into what are the other things we can do in addition to this budget to make this a huge success? We spent the next few days working up our plan. In the end we didn't leave the room until we developed some really great goals, including what we called "stretch goals."

From that day forward we launched the Charter Michigan Blizzard and created the opportunity for people to belong to something. I personally attended the kick-off for the Michigan Blizzard at most of our operations offices so the front line team could hear our thoughts about why we were creating a football team. It was well received at every meeting because it was new, fun and showed that we cared about each and every team member's support of the program. They loved it. And from that day forward, all the rest of the stuff you will learn about in this book, such as the daily call, KPIs and all of the other processes, took root out of these meetings.

The bonding that went on at the meeting was intense. Those newly acquired employees came to that meeting with concerns and fears... "What if I lose my job today? What if Charter is going to wipe out the whole management team?" I did hear that later. They came thinking I was going to announce I was bringing in a whole bunch of new people and they were going to be gone. Instead, fear turned to excitement.

As a leader you have to be sensitive and you always have to put yourself in your teammate's shoes. Think about what they are going through and how they will receive what they hear. Think about your audience and how are they going to relate to what you are saying. How would I feel if I were in those chairs? From an early age my father taught me that every person wears a sign on their chest – "make me feel important". I never forgot that. You can call it active listening and you can call it servant leadership. Whatever you call it, in the end it's all about getting everyone engaged and contributing to the success of the organization.

They went from, "How am I going to feed my family?" to "I've got a jersey with my name on it!!!" From that day forward those people knew they had a position on the team and the position was theirs to lose.

You have to allow yourself to be an actor and get into the part – to have fun with it. Yet, while being an actor, you have to maintain your poise and position – in my case as that of a regional vice president and coach.

What I did was set the foundation that it was okay to be a little zany, it was okay to be creative and that it was okay to have fun. It wasn't long before that attitude permeated throughout the organization the rest of the time I was there.

Looking back to those other organizations, I wish I would have done it earlier because, if done right, it really brings teams together. The football theme gave us a shared history. Everyone who was there at that meeting remembers that day.

That day changed my life too. You have to remember I was just as scared as they were, except I could not show it.

The same thing happened the following year at Central Cyclone, the St. Louis Central Region. We did the same press meeting. Before I walked in that room I was looking in the eyes of a bunch of INDIVIDUALS. After that kickoff I was looking into the eyes of TEAMMATES - and that's a big difference.

Occasionally I'm asked how this whole thing about the football team came to me.

Before I got in the car to go the airport with Dave I truly was on the edge - did I want to stay at Charter? I have to admit I had a certain amount of frustration that I was even put in that situation. I did not have any of the information I needed; I was brought down to the corporate office for a meeting, in front of a Fortune 500 CEO and put through the meat grinder on stuff I didn't even know. That, to me, felt egregious. Then on the way back to the airport when Dave asked me what I was going to do and I told him I was going to start a football team, it's funny, but that is when everything changed… in that instant it all came together.

On the flight home, I had an incredible sense of peace that settled over me and all kinds of ideas flowed. I started sketching out the way we could actually do it. The next day when I walked into my regional office with our sparse team, I wanted to be able to communicate my vision and why I wanted to start a football team. When I did, I got the same blank stares. It is like walking in and saying I want to start a superhero club! But they all said okay.

Once I spent the time thinking it through I was able to set the stage for my regional team. I knew I had to explain it in such a way that it made sense to them. Here is what I told them…

> There are some really important similarities here. There are four quarters in a year; there are four quarters in a football game. When you get halfway through the year you usually pause for a bit. You take a look at where

you've been and where you are going. You re-forecast and think of the second half of the year, which is much like a football game where there is a half time.

We talk in business about winning and losing, about scoring and making points, about winning the day and about winning the game. All of those things gel very easily and quickly into the concept of a football team in business.

If you step back and take a look at the positions in football, obviously you start with the quarterback. The quarterback in our case was our general managers running the various operations across the state.

In my mind the running back would be the head of marketing that reported to the general manager. Their goal was to move the ball and to grow the operations so they would, to me, make a very easy position of running back.

The offensive line was also what I called the defensive line. Just like the old days of football when the linemen played both offense and defense, our folks in the field who are doing the installations, service calls, maintenance and all those kinds of things are our "linemen." These people are impacting and touching our customers every single day because they are in the trenches.

The wide receivers, to us, were in our customer care operations. Think wide receiver – phone receiver and you'll have it. They are the ones on the phone talking to our customers. This was our team.

We also have coaches –

- Our offensive line coach;
- Our offensive coordinator;

- Our defensive coach;
- Our defensive coordinator
- Our head coach – yep, that was me.

Each organization has supervisors and managers that ran service and maintenance. The offensive coordinator was Rudy Tober, our VP of Marketing for the entire region. His job was to work with the running backs and the quarterbacks and move the ball. He was there to make things happen.

Our defensive coordinator was Rodney Lanham, VP of Technical Operations. Rodney was responsible to oversee the maintenance and service techs to make sure they were all doing the things they needed to do.

I also had a "special teams" coach which was Dave Gilles, my VP of Fiscal Operations. Dave's job was to handle accounting, budgeting and all the special kind of things that go on in the business that are absolutely necessary. Just like in football, your special teams can actually win the game for you at the end of the day. So we created the coaching layers and the teams. My senior management team and I had all that stuff thought-out and "cooked up" before we went to the meeting with the employees.

We were so organized that I not only gave each teammate a jersey with their name on the back, but I told them what their position was and on what team they played. They knew specifically what they were going to do, what we expected of them and what they needed to achieve.

During that fateful plane ride home, I sketched out most of the concept and then my regional team and I flushed more of it out over the next few days.

As a leader it is important to commit yourself to something. Once you commit yourself...

Let me use a football analogy. It's like when Joe Namath committed himself and the New York Jets to beating the Baltimore Colts in Super Bowl III. I watched when Namath said,

> Yeah I was at a press dinner and when I said it I put a tremendous amount of pressure and stress on my team and myself. But we were committed; we had to do it...

So when I told Dave Barford I was going to form a football team I was committed - I was all in. Now I had to figure out how to do it and how to get my team on board so I didn't look like an idiot.

I'm sure Dave probably went home that night and completely forgot about it and thought it was probably a moment of idiocy because the guy was scared out of his mind. But to me, I was committed.

Key Take-Aways from Chapter 2

- Be creative. It's fun. Go ahead and get out there and do something challenging. Get out of your 'comfort zone'. You and your team will benefit in the end.
- Put yourself in your teammate's shoes. You need to understand where they are coming from. What motivates them? Why are they on your team? Just like selling a product's features and benefits to a potential customer you need to explain the features of your organization and the resulting benefits that result for each teammate so they can connect the dots and have a better understanding and drive 'buy-in'.
- Plan, plan, plan. Plan your work and work your plan.
- Be committed. Your teammates will be able to tell if you aren't. That's critical!

- Make everyone feel important. They are....show them how they are!

Interviews with Team Members and Partners

At that time, I was living in Florida working for another firm. A recruiter contacted me; I interviewed over the phone and eventually accepted the job as the Regional Director of Customer Care with Charter Communications in Michigan.

A few days before New Year's 1999, I flew from Orlando to Detroit and then on to Muskegon, Michigan. When I left Orlando, it was 80 degrees and ended up flying into a blizzard in Muskegon.

The airline told me that my flight from Detroit to Muskegon was very questionable. They weren't sure if they could take off, and if so, they weren't sure they could land in Muskegon! So I said "that's fine, I'll rent a car and drive since my first day on the job was tomorrow. Well, they said", we can't get you your suitcase!" I couldn't go without my clothes, so I decided I would take the flight.

Now I don't like to fly, but I got on the plane and flew from Detroit to Muskegon, not knowing whether or not we could land. The pilot circled and circled, then finally landed. I grabbed my luggage and soon realized that I had brought Florida clothes, not upper Michigan clothes!

The next morning I arrived at this really small call center. I met Bill and Sherry Olds, who was our HR person, and started right then.

Bill was essentially building the management team from scratch. There were 5 separate cable companies that had been acquired and were operating completely independently of each other. At the time, I believe, I was the second or third person who was hired. Since then, my life has never been the same!

Terie Hannay
Past Regional Vice President, Customer Care,
Charter Communications, Michigan

Interview with Team Members and Partners

> Bill surprised me when I asked him what he was going to do to make this budget happen by basing his success on creating a football team. While I was looking at it from a very tactical perspective, Bill looked at the bigger strategic vision of pulling his people into a common platform they could all compete from and make it a success. I hadn't seen it done before, so I was a bit skeptical at first.
>
> **Dave Barford, past Charter Communication's COO and Senior Vice President of Charter Communication's Western Division**

> Bill and I met in July/August 1985. At the time, I was the telemarketing manager for American Cable Systems, and Bill was hired as the Region Controller. From 1985, both of our careers evolved in the cable industry. There were times when we worked together and other times we didn't, but our friendship remained throughout the years.
>
> Bill and I first met at meetings, going out to lunch, and working with our small regional team. We soon found we had many interests in common such as family and sports, and our friendship soon developed.
>
> As our controller, Bill was fun, a great guy, straight forward and personable. When Bill became a GM, he brought me back from Cape Cod to Romeoville as his operations manager in 1993 or 1994. As the Operations Manager I had Customer Service and the Payment Center. It's funny now to think that our offices were connected via a bathroom!
>
> At the time, we had about 65,000 customers. By the time I left, we had over 100,000 subscribers.
>
> Bill was also successful developing political relationships, which had soured with the prior management. Once people met Bill, they immediately warmed up, and many wanted to work for Bill! To me, that speaks volumes of the type of manager and person he is.
>
> Bill's style has always been to think of, and treat his employees as, a team. He has a "let's work together and find a solution attitude", and is also very family focused. That's a rare attitude with most other management styles.
>
> **Frank Scotello –**
> **Disney, past Vice President of National Accounts**

Interview with Team Members and Partners

> Bill and I started working together at Suddenlink, where I was the Chief Accounting Officer. In our 2nd life together, I was the CFO, and by now we have worked closely together for 9+ years.
>
> From a historical perspective, Bill and I have worked together on three businesses; Suddenlink, Broadstripe and now Pulse Broadband. As Bill said in the past, there is a reason he keeps bringing me back, but more importantly, there is also a reason I keep coming back. Long ago, I bought into his philosophy.
>
> It is interesting to see how the culture Bill creates plays a real role in the success of these organizations Bill has been involved with.
>
> Culturally, we do things like show up to meetings early - and prepared. In a real sense, the people in Bill's team take their jobs very seriously. What I think is unique, is that people don't take themselves too seriously. This creates a light atmosphere in how we all interact with each other. But when it comes to the mission, we are really serious about it and there is an incredibly high level of professionalism. We are very professional on one hand and then on a personal level we can have fun and kind of give it to each other.
>
> What Bill does is a real art.
>
> When we joke around with each other it is always in fun, but no one is making a joke of the business. When it comes to business, we are all serious. There is no "thank God it's Friday" or "oh well we will get to it tomorrow" mentality. There are also the boundaries around our joking and kidding, and that part of it is constructive and a big piece of the puzzle culturally.
>
> **Mike Wylie, past Suddenlink CAO, CFO Broadstripe and current CFO Pulse Broadband**

Interview with Team Members and Partners

I guess it was late 1999 when Dave Barford hired Bill to run the Michigan Region, which was a conglomerate of 2-3 separate acquisitions. All the acquisitions were dispersed companies. There was not a lot of investment in the businesses, nor a clear focus. Bill's job was to bring these acquisitions together under one roof and make it all work.

Bill's first all-team meeting was up in Michigan. I was a Divisional Head of Operations and Finance guy, so Bill and I worked for the same boss. Bill saw the Divisional and Corporate roles as partners, not adversaries, and both were resources that could help him achieve his Regional goals.

My first exposure to Bill's football theme was the Michigan Blizzard Football kick off meeting.

Dave Barford and I attended the meeting. It was electrifying and energizing and Bill had a completely different way to look at building a team. At that meeting, Bill worked with his management team to set goals and priorities, and to build a philosophy that basically overarched everything else. It didn't take years to pull it all together and develop a well-oiled machine. That was accomplished within a couple of months and then business really took off.

Jim Holanda, CEO – RCN/Choice Cable

CHAPTER THREE
BUILDING YOUR PLAN AND KPIs

Too often we fall into the same patterns every day. We get up at the same time, go to work at the same time and follow the same patterns when we get to work. Without even thinking we begin today the same way we did yesterday.

Of course, business meetings and travel change our patterns a bit. Even when that happens, it's human nature to want to get back to our comfortable routines – as quickly as we can.

But to create a winning team and a winning organization, the first thing you have to do is to come up with unique and different ways how to identify that today is different from yesterday. Change keeps things fresh and keeps us from developing unproductive habits. Only then can you keep the organization heading in the right direction.

In other words you have to:

- Set daily and weekly goals,
- Monitor the goals,
- Measure the goals,
- Make adjustments and take corrective actions when goals are missed,
- Rejoice in the goals when they are achieved, and
- Celebrate the accomplishments on a regular basis.

Since 1988 I have used the same Mission Statement at every organization I had the responsibility to manage. My teams have always used it to make the big decisions that face every company. Here it is again, simple but effective:

- <u>Take care of the customer</u> – Always provide excellent customer care at all touch points
- <u>Take care of each other</u> – Always provide excellent support for our team members by creating a great place to work that is challenging and personally rewarding
- <u>Do what we say we we're going to do</u> – This is a biggie! We meet or exceed ALL of our goals and keep our word, always.
- <u>Celebrate</u> – Celebrate our success in meaningful ways. That's right….have fun!

Identifying that we needed to make work more fun and get our team mates flowing with production and creativity is what led us to using a football theme. Keeping with the NFL football theme we started off by acknowledging that

- We want to win the "division" this year,
- We want to win the "conference" next year, and
- We want to win the "Super Bowl" in year three.

Following up on these "wants", we defined SPECIFICALLY what we had to do to win the division, the conference and the Super Bowl. Through this process we were able to get people to come to work every day and feel they were an integral and important part of the game; part of the process and part of the success.

It wasn't good enough to just show up, do your thing and go home. With our approach, you are part of something bigger. What we were able to convey was that we were all part of an organization that was looking to win every game and for the team to become a dynasty.

Let's set the stage with how we did this. Yea, I know, you might be thinking right about now that this whole thing is a bit hokey. Ok, I'll grant you that on the surface it might be. But there is nothing "surface" about what we did. The football theme provided the platform – the playing field, if you will - on which we built a world class operational organization.

Think of this in terms of a football team. What would a football team do and how would a head coach go about building a future Super Bowl team? Now, keep that image in mind as we go through the next parts of this process.

One of the first things a head coach does is to sit down in the quiet of his own office and begin to map out what he wants to accomplish. Then he takes an initial look at his personnel so that he can determine the teams' overall strengths and weaknesses.

Yea, I've been saying "he" because as of yet, there aren't any female head coaches of a pro team but that doesn't mean female executives, managers and supervisors can't do the same thing. There are lots of incredible female athletes, coaches and trainers. So for the time being, I'm going to stay with the "he" references but will switch to the he/she references when it is appropriate for the storyline.

After the head coach assesses what he has, he then meets with his coaching staff to get their ideas, input, critiques and suggestions. Collectively they set offensive and defensive goals as well as goals for each special team. Once the overall gameplan is on paper and everyone is on the same page it is time for each member of the coaching staff to work with the players to execute each and every part of the gameplan.

In business it is the same process; we just call it by different names. So what I did was to add football descriptions to each part of the process. That worked for me because it is how I thought. To me it wasn't hokey - it was how I got things done with my "team."

The first thing that a coaching staff does when preparing for a game is to review recent game films of the team you are about to play. You analyze how they play, their strengths and their weaknesses. You study their offensive line and strategies as well as their defensive line and strategies. You identify patterns that they play and plays that they like to execute. You watch how their special teams play and analyze the effectiveness of their execution. You also watch the coaches, get as much Intel as you can about the players and bundle all that up into what business calls a competitive review.

Then the coaches sit down and meet as a team. In our case, we had the daily call with all my coaches. I 'm sure you are wondering how would you find time to get anything done if you have to talk with the region or corporate staff every day!?! I can tell you from experience that when you focus on **WHAT IS IMPORTANT TO WINNING** in your organization, you get "hearts and minds" on the daily call and you can get the call down to less than 30 minutes. Isn't winning in your organization worth 30 minutes of your time every day? When appropriate, we also had the individual players (I mean front line personnel in addition to management) on the call so we could get important information and perspectives firsthand. I usually managed the calls by including all operations management in the region. Everyone on the call, whether local or across the country, was intimately involved in what we were trying to achieve.

During our call we had a spreadsheet with about 10 key things we wanted to really focus on. When we got on the phone we talked about those 10 key things. We focused on where each person was to his or her goals. It was through this process that my management team and I could tell who was moving the ball, who fumbled the ball and who scored a touchdown. We knew exactly what happened because we broke the process down into very small pieces so we could all measure our actions, our fumbles and our successes. Better yet, everyone in our operating units knew how they were performing and knew that everyone else did too. This alone can be quite a motivator.

All of these critical key items became known as our **KEY PERFORMANCE INDICATORS** or KPIs.

You probably are wondering how we settled upon 10 KPIs for our calls. Here is how it happened. We really ended up breaking it down into two pieces.

First, I used my experience in cable to identify what are the key things we were looking to measure. For example, in video we needed to know things like:

- What was the net customer gain per day (connects less disconnects)?
- What was our churn rate (percentage of customers leaving us and why)?

Then we broke that down even further into video, data and phone. With this approach, we knew what the net gain goal is today.

Let's say that we wanted to grow 100 customers in this region each day. Using this approach, tomorrow on our morning call we would say how many new customers did you get yesterday? Let's assume the manager's answer was 95. The next question was "what happened to the other five? What is your plan to make up that 5 today? How did your connects compare to your disconnects"? If they had 200 connects and 100 disconnects they hit their net gain goal but all of that activity indicates there is a deeper problem – why are we losing 100 customers!?! Just like most businesses it is easier to keep a customer than to gain a new one and most likely less expensive too.

That's one piece of it.

The other piece of the process was to look at the Key Performance Indicators. The Key Performance Indicators are what we identified as the "key" things that would drive our business growth.

In the cable business, one business item that is huge is what is known as "drop buries." A "drop bury" is when an installer comes to your house or place of business, rolls out the cable from the pole to your house and then leaves the cable laying on top of the yard. This happens mostly in the winter but it is one of the highest drivers of dissatisfaction for new customers. So you identify the goal of getting drop buries completed in the same day or no later than the next day. This is the kind of minutia you need to identify in your KPIs, which in turn drives business growth.

Every business owner, executive, manager and employee knows that customer satisfaction is a key element of business growth. Since that is the case, how can customer satisfaction not be part of your KPIs? It absolutely must be, which is why customer satisfaction KPIs are a crucial component of driving business growth.

In our case, we called our phone center customer relations staff our Customer Advocates and, you guessed it, the Customer Advocates had their own KPIs. For us the Customer Advocates were the voice of the customer. We would often have one or two of them join us in a staff meeting, give us their perspectives first hand and tell us what they think. It's also ego-bruising but it made better managers and operators out of each one of us.

To accomplish all of this, each region created the Daily Subscriber report which was an excel file for each region or business unit. Each operation sent these to our regional headquarters so we could summarize all the information on one page. I took these reports and forwarded them back to my managers so everyone on the call had that information right in front of them.

These reports were very dynamic and helped the business dramatically. I was managing 13 states so I could say, "Nebraska your goal was to gain 345 video customers and you gained 240, so tell me what happened?"

For example, they might tell me that they had an ice storm. So okay your net gain goal today was going to be 150 but now it is 300 because we have new customers in the pipe we didn't get done yesterday so we are going to make up yesterday and today and get a bigger number. We would then ask "what resources do you need to get this done" showing them that we were serious about them getting their numbers and offering whatever assistance we could. That's the kind of dynamic that happened each and every day.

I think this is the time for an important note on managing. I never found it helpful to belittle or verbally climb on a manager on the call. If I needed to dress someone down for whatever reason, I always did it privately in a one on one call or meeting. On the call, I've always believed it was important to stay positive and focused.

There were many days when that was very tough to do. I might have had lots of pressure from above but I've never believed in publicly humiliating anyone. It was never my style. I would ask someone to stay on the line after the call because they didn't have the right answers and that was usually enough to get everyone's attention. I didn't have to dress them down because those scary words *"please stay on after the call"* said it all to everyone else on the call.

We sometimes had calls with 13 states and had anywhere from 3-10 people from each state. Sometimes there were over 100 people on the call but the leader of the call was directly responsible for driving that business unit. Usually it was the general manager who was speaking for that business unit. The GM's staff that was part of the call never wanted to be the source of a less than desirable report for their GM.

Sometimes the cable business can get confusing so let's try another example. If you are a Tupperware manufacturer, you make plastic bowls. How many plastic bowls do you want to sell in 2012? A second question might be how many do you want to sell each quarter and then break it down even farther to each month, week and day. Another question could be how do you identify how you are you going to get that done? Who is responsible for each part of the process? Who orders the materials to manufacture your products? How much material do you need on hand to meet or exceed your goals? What important parts of each process do you need to track?

In other words, you continue to drill-down until you get to the key elements of what drives your business as well as each part of the process. That way, you can make sure you have the right people responsible to drive the process forward. Once you identify the person who drives that part of the bus then you identify each part of the daily process so that you can know how it is going every day.

These daily calls didn't take too long and shouldn't take more than 15 to 30 minutes. What's terrific about all this is that once you identify the key activities for each part and process of your organization, you are golden. Again, this is time well spent. If you are all located in the same building hold a quick huddle and meet together. I learned early in my career that nothing beats hearing directly from your front line team what is happening. Otherwise the "Mushroom Theory of Management" (keep upper management in the dark and keep piling on the crap) can take hold in your organization. Not good.

The KPIs identify specifically what you should be talking about. Get on the call, focus on the KPIs, rally the troops and let them go do their job. Don't lecture, don't micromanage and don't bring the team down. Let the KPIs do the talking and keep the managers and staff focused. When the KPIs become their yardstick, the managers and staff know it – and over half of your work is done.

This is true whether your company is selling books, selling consulting services or coaching a pro football team.

Back to the Tupperware manufacturer; we need to sell 300 bowls each week in the month of January in order to get a first down. That's a total of 1200 bowls for January and 3,600 bowls for the first quarter which gives us a touchdown. You can score each touchdown with 6 points so you have 4 quarters X 6 points = 24 points at year end. You can come up with fun ways to get extra points too, e.g. more bowls sold over budget, etc. Believe me; you can actually define it this way! It works and we created a lot of enthusiasm with this approach.

Each team member needs to know "what does it mean to win?" One manager might say, "Okay, I hit the number of bowls that I was supposed to sell. I made the quarter and I made a touchdown! That's 6 points!"

This is a key subject that I hope you learn if you don't learn anything else from this book. All of us business leaders need to identify what it means to win in our organization. If you can't succinctly detail your mission in three sentences or less you may have a problem. You are the leader. If you don't have clarity about where your organization needs to go, no one else will know either. Your team is looking for you to show them the way. Be clear. Be succinct. Be aggressive. And then measure, measure, measure and finally celebrate!

Figure out how many points (products) you have to score (sell) to beat your competitors. Figure out what your competitors are doing. You have to understand your competitor - the other team. That's how you drill-down to the lowest common denominator.

Doing that allows you to really accelerate your business, your profits and your excitement about life, then measure it. Statistics are like a GPS tracking system. They tell you where you are all the time, how far you are from your goal, are you staying on track and how far you have deviated from your route.

Focus on the KPIs you develop and like a GPS, those KPIs will lead you to the Red Zone and then to the goal line. Your job, if you chose to accept it, is to keep pushing the ball along that path and keep driving forward until you cross the goal line and score!

Key Take-Aways from Chapter 3

- Embrace Change. It's going to happen so get ahead of it!
- Set goals. You won't know where you end up if you don't know where you want to go.
- Have a clear and concise Mission Statement – What is yours?
- Daily call = winning
- Key Performance Indicators. You can expect what you inspect. So true.
- What does it mean to win in your company? How do you know if you are winning?

Daily call suggestions:

- All senior team members, from all regions, participate on a regularly scheduled call with the corporate team every day at 3:00 CST.
- Utilize a formatted daily call report
- At the beginning of each month the teams forecast their connects, disconnects, and net gain for their products. On the daily call the teams report work (net gain) completed the day before compared to forecast, forecasted work sent to the field for installation or disconnect that day and forecasted work for the next day. We discuss marketing tactics and look for ways to support the team.
- Every Wednesday we review the KPIs with each of the teams. Review prior month results early in the month and review current month's forecast weekly.
- On average the call takes 10 to 30 minutes for completion with high impact results. Everyone on the team understands what is important and we reinforce this message daily.

Interviews with Team Members

> At that point, I wasn't always a participant in Bill's daily calls and meetings but Bill always included us in terms of weekly or monthly updates. During those updates, we at Division got a better understanding of how he was using the Michigan Blizzard team and philosophy to achieve his corporate goals.
>
> **Jim Holanda, CEO – RCN/Choice Cable**

> Years later when Bill got the call to become a Divisional head and run the home market of St. Louis; I got a lot more exposure to his process.
>
> Bill asked me to be the Area VP and work for him directly. That was my first major field operations role and it was all pretty overwhelming. I was a young guy at the time and having to take on this task with 1800 employees from day one was a real stretch, and at times overwhelming. But Bill was very reassuring and a calming leader. He was a great mentor and explained that we were going to follow the same highly successful thematic leadership approach he used in Michigan.
>
> The doubt and anxiety went away when I embraced all of Bill's fundamental leadership principles. Bill's unique approach to team building and running the business by the numbers on a day to day basis really works. In fact, it has become such a successful formula for me over the last 12 years, that I've used it ever since.
>
> What I will proudly say is that by following Bill's approach, I know I accomplished more in those two years than I ever thought I could. And that continues to this day…
>
> **Jim Holanda, CEO – RCN/Choice Cable**

Interviews with Team Members

> What Bill does is a little bit different than many of the businesses with which I have been involved. He uses this KPI program not just as a tool – but also as a platform to discuss all the goals of the business. The KPIs are the "how" are we doing - the mission statement is "what" we are doing. That's the key; there are a lot of different discussions and processes that spring from all these metrics.
>
> Most of the organizations that I have worked with in the past have had some level of performance indicators, but they are not nearly as dispersed.
>
> When Bill's KPI program was implemented, the people executing their respective KPIs became walking encyclopedias of their numbers. We are not talking on a monthly basis; but on a daily or weekly basis. You could walk up to a mid-level manager and ask how were their "connects" today, or what is their service call rate? These guys knew it down to the nth degree. That is pretty unique.
>
> I've seen performance indicators used in the past. However, the programs were a lot less sophisticated and the only folks that knew and understood the KPIs were the very top leaders of the program.
>
> I had one client that had a lot of retail stores across the country. The CEO knew what each store was supposed to produce. When a store would miss their goals, he would bolt out of his office, call the team and either berate or talk to them about what they need to do better. Because his performance numbers were not always clearly spelled out, there was mystery behind what was expected.
>
> Bill's KPI approach takes the mystery out of it, and brought the numbers to life without big bonuses and big threats. The way Bill has perfected it, he's put a fun program around it, theme based, sport based program which gets people to interact. It works really well, particularly in geographically dispersed organizations.
>
> **Mike Wylie, past Suddenlink CAO, CFO Broadstripe and current CFO Pulse Broadband**

Interview with Team Members

> The folks that showed up for meetings in their jerseys whooping and carrying on were the guys who would consistently win. I don't think anyone pushed back on the program, but the guys who really got excited about it were generally more successful.
>
> **Mike Wylie, past Suddenlink CAO, CFO Broadstripe and current CFO Pulse Broadband**

> In addition to the KPIs, the interaction of the daily call was really helpful.
> When you find an issue you want to drill into, KPIs help management to understand why something has happened relative to what your expectations. That's a big part of the power of the combination of the KPIs and Daily Call.
>
> It really is something how this works, particularly when you have regions across the country that are isolated or operate as silos. Within literally weeks, not months of implementing something like this, these guys are talking to one another, on the same phone calls, they would use the KPI phone calls to share best practices.
>
> From a management perspective, KPIs are also a great way to benchmark one regions performance against another. The process quickly sheds light on who is doing well and who is falling behind. The organization also benefits from all the data and best practices sharing. What Bill has developed is more a platform approach than a tool, and he has done exceptionally well over the years with his
> system.
>
> **Mike Wylie, past Suddenlink CAO, CFO Broadstripe and current CFO Pulse Broadband**

Interviews with Team Members

> I don't think there is ever any question and to a degree it is unspoken; our families are the priority. That's not to say we haven't missed some soccer games in peak times, but whenever possible, our families remain our priority.
>
> First of all, each of us had a real sincere interest for each other's kids and families.
>
> If someone says they have to be there for their kids whatever, it is just unspoken; we went. It's in the mission statement and it's not lip service.
>
> It was, and remains, an incredible priority for everyone.
>
> **Mike Wylie, past Suddenlink CAO, CFO Broadstripe and current CFO Pulse Broadband**

Interview with Team Members

About 4 months in, we had finally pulled together most of the plan, including its primary goals and objectives. Our focus was on understanding what operational assets we had, what our talent was and the additional members we had to hire.

As the team was starting to build, Bill rolled out his Michigan Blizzard football theme. We did a kick off around early March of 2000 at a hotel and the entire team got their jerseys. Bill had us put on our jersey's right then and he kicked off the football team.

I think initially, the entire room was like a "deer in the head lights." We all kind of looked at each other with a "what is this?" and "what am I supposed to do with this?" look on our faces.

Here we all were, a bunch of people in suits wanting to make a good impression on the new Regional Vice President. And there's Bill in a football jersey! It was definitely "deer in the head lights" time! I know it was for me!

But it certainly didn't take Bill long to get us to understand his football theme. As he kicked it off, Bill said, "This is the team and we've got a name. Here's our goal!" And he laid it all out. Bill introduced his KPI concepts and told us about how some of this was going to be measured. He told us how we were going to win, how it would be tracked and tied it all to his football theme.

Even though none of us had ever seen anything like this from a business perspective, I don't think there was a person in the room that really couldn't grasp the correlation.

Terie Hannay
Past Regional Vice President, Customer Care, Charter Communications, Michigan

Interview with Team Members

> Obviously we had a number of women at the call center, and many were unfamiliar with football. But as long as the jersey fit, they were in!
>
> Of course, many of the ladies were hesitant at first. Most of us didn't really know much about football, but everybody knows what a touchdown is.
>
> Soon, everyone got it – and that football was how we were going to track the metrics, and hit our goals. Once the people understood that, the group became a cohesive team; it clicked and things were fine.
>
> **Terie Hannay**
> **Past Regional Vice President, Customer Care, Charter Communications, Michigan**

CHAPTER FOUR

THE KICK-OFF, GO LIVE WITH YOUR PLAN

In football, the kickoff creates a sense of urgency and excitement. All too often, particularly in important games like playoffs, nerves get the better of players and their performance suffers.

To counter that, thoroughly understanding your competition often helps reduce the jittery performance early in the game. Fear of the unknown can be offset with training and knowing what to expect from your opponent. Performance is also improved because fewer mistakes are made when we know what our competition is likely to do in a given situation.

> Some concern about a team can be mitigated by putting together a gameplan based on the strengths and weaknesses observed on video as well as the strengths and weakness of individual players.
>
> The main use of game films is to hopefully determine some tendencies on offense and defense given down, distance, position on the field and score of the game. Observing the actions of players that immediately affect your position and your play, gives you some indication what to expect. However, as a player and as a team, we need to keep in mind that our opponent is most likely anticipating us making some obvious adjustments, so we have to be smart about how we utilize what we think we know.
>
> The job of the coaching staff is to put together a gameplan, utilizing our strengths while keeping in mind what the other team is anticipating...sort of like a chess match putting these gameplans together.
>
> The reason they kept running that play is because they always made yardage on it. When the tight end took a 3 yard split that power sweep was coming...but there was always the chance the defense was being set up, so the defense had to play it straight every time.
>
> JACKIE'S PERSPECTIVE

Thanks Jackie, the same thing happens in business. But first you have to start with asking several important questions:

- How do you define winning, and
- What are your goals?

Some companies can answer these questions right away and some can't.

What's important is to develop the answers with laser clarity. The coaches and managers must know who their team is, who their competitor is, what are their goals and what strategies and tactics are included in their "gameplan preparation."

Once those questions are answered, the next step is to know your team and its capabilities. I'm talking about a team assessment – of its strengths and challenges.

If their hearts are in the right place and they want to succeed, you then look at their strengths. You may not be able to do this strategy because it doesn't play to your strengths. However, with a few modifications then you can do this because it plays completely to your strengths. For example, a better alternative for you might be baseball or soccer.

This is a great place to introduce what I call the "Evolution of Winning". There are four steps that get you from zero to hero. They are:

I Can't

When you are looking to improve your organization and you are working to instill pride and a sense of winning into your team, very often you will hear teammates say that they can't do their job.

What they are usually saying is that there are some tools they are missing that keep them from being successful.

It could be equipment issues, e.g. a cable TV installer needs a working meter to make sure that signal levels are correct before they complete the installation. Some companies cut corners and don't provide the necessary equipment teammates need to do their job. This would be like telling a tackle to take on a defensive lineman without the proper shoulder pads. It may be the need to provide training or some other program. Whatever the case, listen to your team and work hard to understand what they really need. They may have the best intentions but they can't do the job without the right equipment. If you want to show your team that you are serious about winning, you need to supply the tools to do the job. If you don't, your team will soon see you as a dreamer or worse, a liar. Put your money where your mouth is. You will buy incredible good will from your team if you support them. Keep your "antennae" up too. Your teammate may not want to do the job and will not perform regardless of the tools and training you provide. **Know when to make the needed team cuts; your remaining team will thank you.** When you address these issues you help your team move into the "I Can"

I Can

OK, now you have your team believing that they can do their job. You have them properly equipped, trained and they are ready to go. When teammates say they can do their job you have made good progress but you are far from fielding the winning team you desire. Just because someone can do a job doesn't mean they will perform at a high level. In fact, without the proper motivation, people begin to do their job in a rote manner. Every day is the same as yesterday, last week and last month. They think 'no one is watching and no one seems to care if I perform at a high level or if I just meet the minimum requirements'. 'I can do the job.....I'm just not sure that I want to'. This is still a bad place to be for a company that wants to be a future contender for major market share. Leaders have to know how to get the team to the next level, provide direction and share goals in a clear and concise manner. The platform of I Can is necessary as you show the team where you all are headed. You must get them to believe in the mission and make them feel like they are a part of the team. Their job is *important* and *critical* to achieve the mission. They must have input and give their thoughts about how the team will achieve the goal. Without their input, the job will be exactly that....a job. In later chapters we will investigate how to get your team's feedback and buy in; again, a critical step. Once you have their belief your team moves into a really great place....."I Will".

I Will

We can't emphasize enough how important the I Will level is to a team. Now you have hearts and minds. This is a really cool place to be. If you can get your team to take on the mind set of 'the mission will not fail because of me' or better yet 'the mission will be successful because of me', then you are way down the path to becoming a highly functioning team. Remember, you have already ensured that you have A players with the right skill sets to not only play, but to win. The I Will leads to the:

I DID!!

You did it! You hit/beat your goals! It is time to celebrate. It is important to take the time to not only notice your accomplishments but to have some fun and celebrate in a way that your team won't soon forget. We will give you some ideas how you can achieve this later in the book. Again, enjoy the moment! You are a winner!!

You're never going to have a team that is perfect at everything. With that in mind, we need to devise a strategy that will help you move the ball down the field based on your strengths and the tactics that you are really good at executing. You want to make sure that your team is always in the "I Will" stage!

The key is that you assess your team and come up with plays that fit your team's abilities and those are the plays that you run. Vince Lombardi ran the power sweep right - and he ran it and ran it and ran it. He knew where his team's strength was and where the defense was weak and he kept running it and running it.

> Good coaches find ways to utilize the talent of their players. Some coaches put together a gameplan, blocking assignments, pass patterns and if they were to go to another team, they would bring along those same plays. Their basic approach is that these plays, blocked this way, should work and they will if every player is capable of blocking the way it was drawn up. When it comes to blocking assignments there may be several ways to utilize the blockers to accomplish the anticipated result. But some coaches may not take into account each blockers ability to execute the block as the play is designed. Good coaches like Coach Landry took this into account by knowing the other team's players' abilities and so he constructed blocking assignments based on the defender's tendencies and weaknesses and the strengths of the offensive player assigned to block him. By differing from other offenses where plays are drawn up as "the way" to block a play without considering the individual abilities and weaknesses, Coach Landry's attention to detail won Dallas a lot of games. Smart coaches take into account these small but significant observations and insert them into the gameplan, and often tailor them for the team they are playing.
>
> ### JACKIE'S PERSPECTIVE

That reminds me that under the subset of "know your team", make sure you give everyone on your team a position. Like I noted earlier, when we had our championship teams, we actually gave people positions. The General Manager was quarterback, marketers were running backs, and customer care people were wide receivers. Everyone played to their positions and we found that it added to the enjoyment and excitement.

> It simply relates to a coaches ability to determine the depth of a player's talent and utilize it…although not particular to his assigned and expected contribution. For instance, as I think I mentioned Coach Landry saw me throwing the football one day and saw that I could throw it a good distance. From that he constructed a play that would be put in the Super Bowl at the right time. I would leave my tight end position running through the backfield to the right, the QB would pitch me the ball, I would look for the end now running down the far left side and just throw it as far as I could letting the end run under the ball. It was just a one shot deal, taking advantage of something the other team had no way of anticipating.
>
> The simple theme of work ethic is a subtle one but in football it becomes obvious who the hard workers are because of the nature of our participation. You can see if someone is working hard in practice; if he encourages teammates and does the necessary physical and mental preparation to get ready for a game. In the business setting, team members will be successful to the extent of their commitment and the manager's ability to observe and cultivate that commitment.
>
> ## JACKIE'S PERSPECTIVE

That's a great point, Jackie, player and employer commitment and creativity is crucial to the plan's success.

People like to feel like they are contributing and are motivated when someone else notices. As a leader, if you go out of your way to make all your teammates feel important and feel like they are contributing, you are going to change their life dramatically. Do that and most players or employees will do anything they can for the organization.

> When you are asked to do something that has some importance attached to it whether it is a coach, parent or a manager, it conveys to the individual they must be capable or the person in authority would not have asked. A lot of confidence comes from that implied confidence.
>
> If you, as a team member, are out there working really hard, somebody will figure that out. That work ethic is great for contributing to the team's success. However, it is also contributing to the psyche of the players and the team. If I do the right thing and work hard they will figure it out, appreciate it and work hard too.
>
> **JACKIE'S PERSPECTIVE**

Let's build on that point, Jackie. How did Coach Landry do things in different ways than you were used to when you played in St. Louis? Did Coach Landry really build his plays around individual player's strengths and if so, how did he do that?

> Absolutely that is what he did.
>
> I watched him do that as far as changing the blocks we used. When I went to the Dallas Cowboys in 1978, I was able to modify a block in a different way than they did. Coach let me block that way but he had the other tight ends block in their normal way.
>
> As I mentioned before, one day I was on the field throwing the football around. I always had a pretty good arm and he saw me throw the ball quite far so he developed a play that he put in for the Super Bowl, though we never ran it. But we had it in there simply because of how I threw the ball.
>
> The play was that I was going to be pulling a reverse around the back field. The QB was going to pitch me the ball. The outside receiver on the same side heads down field and tries to run by the corner back and down the far side lines. I was going to stop and throw the ball down the field as far as I could.
>
> It was a one shot deal and he had several plays like that where it was all or nothing - a touchdown or nothing.
>
> **JACKIE'S PERSPECTIVE**

Usually you have an offensive coach that puts these kinds of plays together but Coach Landry put them together himself.

He was so good at picking up on the tendencies of the defensive guys. He also put together plays on the real time game basis. Most of the plays were based on what he identified as the individual's tendencies on the field.

Most of us think of X's and O's on the blackboard as guys playing these different offensive and defensive positions; not to Coach Landry. To him they were individuals who reacted differently when they saw certain things on offense so he developed strategically well designed plays. In many cases, it was the small things he knew these guys would do and what their reaction might be depending upon what they saw.

JACKIE'S PERSPECTIVE

For all the time, 15 years, I played with the Cardinals; no coach ever suggested I throw the football in a game. This small example of Coach Landry thinking out of the box was what I originally noticed about him in the two Pro Bowl games I played where he was the coach.

In these games we only have a few plays and they have to be simple and familiar as we only have a couple of days to put together an offense. Coach Landry made the most of the time he had by designing a play for **what he knew about the players we were playing against.** He was familiar with their tendencies and what their reactions would be to what they saw on offense…line movement, back field motion, alignment, certain formations, etc. It was like he knew how they were programmed. Coach Landry seemed to instinctively know how each player would react to certain actions, observations by the offense, quickly and precisely explaining his reasoning during the 10 minutes it took him to draw up the entire offense we would be using.

JACKIE'S PERSPECTIVE

As Jackie just said, it comes down to knowing your team. If you are going to be very successful, you have to sit down with each of your team members and understand their strengths and weaknesses. You also need to know what they want to get out of their efforts. It's important to know what motivates them and what makes them successful.

Once you get a sense for who are your best players, who will help you move the ball down the field then you can build your gameplan. The question to keep in mind is "how can these folks help the team and help us win?" Then you can begin to create plays which capitalize on the strength of your team.

Here is an example of a marketing "play." Let's assume that we want to set up a campaign to achieve two objectives. I know it will be successful because we are designing the campaign around the strengths of the people we have on the "field." If the two objectives are new customer growth and increasing the number of movie channels that our existing customers purchase, we needed to have a great installation team to get the installs completed in a timely manner and a strong customer service team that could effectively sell movie channels, using the telephone, to our customers.

Whenever I came to a new team, I always told the team that we would initially go through a process of assessment. I knew I needed to understand what the organization had done in the past; what were their strengths and weaknesses. It was just like reviewing game films.

I talked often about Coach John McKay when he was running the Tampa Bay Buccaneers when they first became a franchise. Coach McKay had a number of seasons when the Bucs never won a game. He was coming off the field and a reporter came up and said, "Coach, what do you think of your team's execution?" He said "I think it is a good idea".

I always used it when I met with a new team to add some levity but to also make the point that there are two types of execution – everyone always got my point! I always said that we are going to start from scratch and review the game films and identify what is working and not working.

Jackie, who was the best coach you saw at matching player's skill-sets to the gameplan?

> It was by far Coach Landry, as he took it on an individual basis and by observing all the players that directly affect the success of a play, he built a tailor made game play for each team based on the ability of the opposing teams players. Add to that the offensive movement that made it impossible for opposing teams to determine any tendencies and the defense that changed the positions of critical players to unfamiliar alignments making them difficult to block.
>
> Short yardage is inside the 20 yard line where the defense usually changes in this critical area. The short yardage plan was always given out at the Thursday team meeting before practice. At my first such meeting I was surprised to see all the coaches sitting with us while we were waiting for Coach Landry to arrive. This included all the line coaches and passing coach, who in my experience with the Cardinals were the ones that drew up the short yardage gameplan. Yet here they were sitting in the meeting with us until Coach Landry finally arrived with the short yardage gameplan and passed it out to the coaches and players. The position coaches always acquiesced to his knowledge base.
>
> JACKIE'S PERSPECTIVE

> I was always convinced that if players could successfully execute each play Coach Landry conceived and put on the gameplan, we would have never lost a game. If a player failed it was only because the players were not able to execute what he had drawn up not because it was not the right play.
>
> **JACKIE'S PERSPECTIVE**

Great point, Jackie, it really does come down to knowing your team.

> Don't get me wrong, both of these men, Coach Coryell and Coach Landry, are both very sincere and very good men. They were both very dedicated to winning and that was obvious to everybody.
>
> Coach Coryell was more of an emotional coach than Coach Landry and although he had a good strategy and smart gameplans, his personality and approach to the game was the spark that we all saw when he arrived in St. Louis. That spark turned into fire on many occasions on the practice field, in meetings and in games. He was unquestionably consumed by winning and did everything he could to transmit that message to his coaches, players and to himself. He was a football man and so was Coach Landry but Coach Landry's approach allowed him to have a more calm and measured application of his considerable talents. Players loved Coach Coryell because it was so obvious he wanted to win and put himself out there to do it. Coach Landry was also loved and respected because the players knew if they executed the plays he called and conducted themselves the way he expected them to, they would win games.
>
> **JACKIE'S PERSPECTIVE**

> Coach Coryell thought that a lot of work would help lead him to be a winner.
>
> It is just a difference in philosophy, but both of them were very good and very inspirational in their own way.
>
> Coach Landry was able to do it for 25 years and still was very effective as a leader and motivator. He was known as the guy who was stoic on the sidelines. His players knew that the chances were 99% that he had put together a gameplan to win the game. All we had to do was execute it. That in itself was a big, big motivator.
>
> Coach Coryell might give you a big speech to fire you up so you would run out on the field and run everybody over. That was effective for a little while. But for me, I found the kind of effect Coach Landry had lasted for the length of the game. It also lasted for his tenure as the Cowboys head coach.
>
> JACKIE'S PERSPECTIVE

That is so well said, Jackie.

I can't tell you how many times I have had teammates tell me they didn't want to let me down. I believe it's because we came together as a team and everyone believed in each other.

As the CEO or head of an organization I always bent over backwards to make sure my teammates knew I had their back. You build that kind of esprit du corps and people just aren't going to let you down.

To Jackie's point, the Cowboys believed Tom Landry knew what he was doing and had the right gameplan.
In business you get the right people and put the right plays in place (marketing plan, right installers, right product suite and pricing). As a leader, you show your team you know what you

are talking about by listening to your teammates and getting their feedback. At the end of the day you make the decisions. You put the right products and processes in place so that your team can stand up straight and say I believe in what we are doing. When they believe in what they are doing, you can climb mountains.

> We knew there was nothing to do but to do it. In other words we had the right direction and the right gameplan. All that was left was to execute.
>
> **JACKIE'S PERSPECTIVE**

Key Take-Aways from Chapter 4

- How do you define winning in your company? This is critical.
- Where are you in the Evolution of Winning? Where is your team?
- How is your work ethic? Are you an example for others to emulate? In a positive way?
- Know your team's strengths and weaknesses. Really know them and build on the strengths and eliminate the weaknesses as best you can.
- Support your team – always! Walk the talk.

Interviews with Team Members and Partners

> Until I got hurt in my third year in St. Louis I was not seriously focused about what I was going to do later in life. I met a Cardinals supporter and told him I thought I could play a little bit longer. So he arranged a few appointments around St. Louis. We went around and had lunch with various companies that he had connections with. They ranged from Goldman Sachs, United Van, Ford, Emerson Electric and a real estate company.
>
> I didn't get it; my dad had been an hourly worker at the Union Bag Paper Company in Savannah. He never put on a tie to go to work. When I would see what he was doing at work, I could understand it and it made sense to me. When I worked at these offices and I would see the cubicles lined up one after another, I didn't get it. I could not see how anybody was producing anything of value.
>
> Then I asked the supporter who was helping me how he made his money"? He said "I have a big printing business and we print the Southwestern Bell telephone directories. We have been very successful there but I have made most of my money in real estate". I asked him how that worked. He proceeded to tell me, and that's when I said "that's what I want to do." That was my introduction into real estate.
>
> **Taz Anderson**
> **Past All American Fullback at Georgia Tech, Tight end St. Louis Cardinals and the Atlanta Falcons**

> What I love about Bill's leadership style is that he has such a "can do" attitude. He never says "can't" and finds a way through his sport teams to bring groups together, create measurable accountability with goals and objectives, creates a fun way to measure success and creates tremendous enthusiasm from his team.
>
> **Dave Barford, past Charter Communication's COO and Senior Vice President of Charter Communication's Western Division**

Interviews with Team Members and Partners

> It starts with the mission statement and its simplicity. Everyone is able to understand and believe in it. The core of the mission statement is to do the right thing for each other and the customer, and to celebrate your successes.
>
> The other key thing that I learned from Bill's operating philosophy is a bias for action.
>
> When you add it all up, your employees have hundreds and hundreds of years of experience. Allowing them to make decisions on their own, and on behalf of the customer, is crucial. Then, by combining that with concentrating on the business fundamentals – the KPIs – it all comes together. It's just like every great sports team – they win by doing the fundamentals correctly. If you can focus on and do the fundamentals correctly, and have a bias for action every minute of every day, you can't help but be successful.
>
> That overall philosophy is the definition of leadership. It causes people to want to come to work every day and do the right thing. When they do, they feel good. But management can't forget to acknowledge and reward their successes. That keeps people doing the right things on behalf of the customer every day.
>
> **Jim Holanda, CEO – RCN/Choice Cable**

Interviews with Team Members and Partners

> We decided to postpone consolidating the billing systems for several months and tackle more pressing problems. About two months after the kickoff meeting, we were able to pull the data from three different billing systems so that we could talk about the data on a daily basis.
>
> The daily call developed after the KPIs, because the call was really intended to look at the KPIs on a daily basis. "How did we do yesterday?" "What is our plan for tomorrow?" Initially, many people were afraid of their KPIs and the daily call. They felt like, "Oh my goodness, these are hard metrics and things on which I am going to be measured." That fear soon went away as we got comfortable with the reports and the numbers.
>
> Of course, most of the management team was familiar with having performance metrics. What was different was being on a call every day to talk about them. We were expected to know our KPIs and understand what's behind the data coming out of the daily reports. In short, each of us was responsible for our own metrics and we needed to be prepared to discuss what was happening.
>
> It was very clear what we needed to do. We knew where we were starting from and where we were going. More importantly, we knew we couldn't do anything until we knew from where we were starting. Surprisingly, a lot of companies actually don't use that. People just do their job to the best of their ability, but most don't have the ability to use a report like we had. They also don't have a measurement system that tells them what they need to do next week.
>
> You could kind of see light bulbs go off when someone finally understood the metrics and what was expected of them. "Okay - that's what this means; that's how it impacts the company; that's how it impacts the customers. Then people started digging in to their own metrics so they could understand them even more... "What's going on in my business unit and how am I going to fix it?"
>
> **Terie Hannay**
> **Past Regional Vice President, Customer Care, Charter Communications, Michigan**

CHAPTER FIVE
FIRST POSSESSION
GAME FILMS AND INITIAL OBSERVATIONS IN REAL TIME

A critical part of the marketing plan is an assessment of the competition. On the field, coaches and teams review game films. In business, we assess the offers, services, advertisements and capabilities of our competition. The goal is to identify what makes the competition "tick". We want to study their offensive and defensive strategies and see how we can out flank or throw a pass over their defensive tactics.

When I'm thinking about reviewing the game film I'm not only thinking about the competition, I'm thinking about how the competition looks and how my organization is performing at several different levels. But prior to this, we were:

- Setting the ground work,
- Defining what winning means,
- Identifying the goals of the organization,
- Understanding what the team looks like, and
- Reviewing how they have been working and performing in the past.

That's the foundation.

Next we need to look at the competition and identify their apparent goals, as well as their strengths and weaknesses. For our team we can use that information to help us set our own goals using key performance indicators (KPIs). From there we can identify the daily specifics on which we want to focus so we can measure the organization and enable it to win.

> Viewing previously played games by your opponent gives you an overview of their team and a detailed look at individual players. The purpose of reviewing these games for the offense is to chart the defenses they use in a variety of down-and-distance situations. For the defense, reviewing game films helps the players know what plays they can expect from the opponents offense in similar situations.
>
> We have to keep in mind however, that our opponents will be anticipating our adjustments, which makes for somewhat of a chess game. Game films, (digital video these days), also give us a close look at individual players, which is a big key in constructing a gameplan or coming up with new plays. Coach Landry really did it all so brilliantly.
>
> The details of execution are important aspects of the game, but the most important one is to lessen the impact of the opposition's talented players.
>
> Outstanding middle linebackers, gifted outside receivers or other players can be game changers - so they are given special attention.
>
> ## JACKIE'S PERSPECTIVE

> By studying those details we can then take advantage of some of the information and begin to formulate plans for our own offense and defense.
>
> What we are looking for is how they line up in a certain down-or-distance situation. At a certain point in the game, they are likely to run this type of play so you try to build your weekly offense and defense from the previous game's film. Then by observing the offensive and defensive lineups you are looking for an indication of what to expect.
>
> ## JACKIE'S PERSPECTIVE

The Gameplan Prep or business and marketing plan is where we are going to sit down and identify specifically what we want each of the team members in the organization to do. The second part then becomes how we are going to measure what they do.

Here is an example:

Weekly KPI Report - Cable TV Operations	Weighted Potential Score	Goal	Result	Score
KPI Category				
Growth				
Basic Connects	0.10	50	60	0.10
Basic Disconnects	0.10	4	2	0.10
Basic Net Gain	0.30	46	58	0.30
HSD Connects	0.10	55	57	0.10
HSD Disconnects	0.10	3	2	0.10
HSD Net Gain	0.30	52	55	0.30
Telephone Connects	0.10	14	15	0.10
Telephone Disconnects	0.10	2	4	0.00
Telephone Net Gain	0.30	12	11	0.00
Commercial Connects	0.10	2	2	0.10
Commercial Disconnects	0.10	0	0	0.10
Commercial Net Gain	0.30	2	2	0.30
Growth Total	2.00			1.60
Financial Statement Management				
EBITDA	1.50	$50,000	$54,000	1.50
Free Cash Flow (OCF - Cap EX)	1.00	$22,000	$23,000	1.00
Revenue	0.75	$120,000	$123,000	0.75

Weekly KPI Report - Cable TV Operations	Weighted Potential Score	Goal	Result	Score
Commercial Revenue	0.25	$8,500	$9,200	0.25
ARPU	0.50	$99.50	$104.00	0.50
Bad Debt	0.25	1.5%	1.75%	0.00
Non-Pays Completed within 60 days	0.25	1.0%	0.75%	0.25
Financial Total	4.50			4.25
Service Levels				
Drop Buries< 30 days	0.15	90.0%	88.9%	0.00
Installation Completion	0.25	92.0%	94.0%	0.25
Average Availability - Service	0.15	92.0%	93.0%	0.15
Average Availability - Install	0.15	94.0%	94.0%	0.15
Trouble Call Response < 24 Hrs	0.15	90.0%	92.0%	0.15
Trouble Call Response < 48 Hrs	0.15	98.0%	99.0%	0.15
Services Total	1.00			0.85
Resource Management				
Technical Overtime	0.20	8.0%	9.0%	0.00
Tech Sales	0.15	2	0	0.00
Fulfillment Productivity (installers and technicians)	0.20	3.7	3.9	0.20
Contractor Job Percentage	0.20	22.0%	24.0%	0.00
Resource Total	0.75			0.20
Plant Maintenance				
Time to outage repair (minutes)	0.30	75	72	0.30
System Reliability 99.99% or greater	0.30	99.99%	99.9%	0.30
Trouble Call % to Basic Customers	0.30	3.0%	2.5%	0.30

Weekly KPI Report - Cable TV Operations	Weighted Potential Score	Goal	Result	Score
Trouble Call % w/in 30 days of install (in-house & Contractor)	0.30	20.0%	18.0%	0.30
Repeat Trouble Call w/in 30 days	0.30	12.0%	11.0%	0.30
Plant Maintenance Total	1.50			1.50
Contact Rate	0.25	52.0%	55.0%	0.00
Total	10.00			8.40
			Grade	B
9.1 to 10 Points = A				
8.1 to 9 Points = B				
7.1 to 8 Points = C				
6.1 to 7 Points = D				
6 and below is failing				

We used those key performance indicators and percent achieved to drive right into the employees year end appraisal. That way, like us, they were able to keep score and knew what their performance appraisal would be at the end of the year. If I'm an employee getting consistent 90%+ then I am going to get the very top end of a merit increase bonus. The employees will also know if they are eligible for "stretch-bonuses" because they know their score and know what they have to do to get the bonus. Likewise, if they were only scoring in the 75% range, they would know that their performance was only mediocre. Being a "C" player would not get them much of anything - and they might not keep their job.

It's important to build your key performance indicators (KPIs) based on what you want your organization to achieve. **It could be 10 or 12 categories but I would definitely keep it**

under 15. Some people want to measure everything, but when you do that, almost everything gets lost in the process! Keep it simple and focused, that way your team is not chasing too many goals. Just like when we were kids, we always wanted to know how something was rated on a scale of 1 to 10 (10 being the best). I used the same thought when we built our KPI weighting process. Let me explain this a little better. There may be 5 major categories that you want to track. Let's assume that Growth is the first, Financial results are second, Customer service is third, Operations is fourth and Inventory control is fifth.

First let's look at Growth. Again, you are measuring everything on a 10 point scale so you need to identify the weighting of each section totaling the 10 points. In the case of growth this may be the most important area of your company so you might assign 3 points to that category. Financial results are always significant so you might assign 2 points. You are trying to improve your customer service operation so you might assign 2 points here as well. You have assigned 7 points so far. You may also be really focused on Operations so you might assign 2 points to that category leaving 1 point for Inventory control. This adds to 10 and allows you the flexibility to change the weighting in the future, if needed. Each of these 5 sections could include 5 or 6 items in each section. You would then give each sub-section a weighting that adds to the total of the section. Again, let me make an example.

Let's use the Financial results section. We have 2 points comprising this section. You may be focused on revenue, expense control, cash flow, bad debt and salaries. You can put weighting on each area based on its importance to the total category e.g. revenue - .5 points, expense control - .3 points, cash flow - .5 points, bad debt - .4 (a potential area of concern for you), and salaries - .3 points. These 5 items total 2 points for the section. **I really like having this weighting system because I can manage the business at a high level AND at a micro level. On a high level I can track the**

monthly performance of the KPIs by watching where we land each month/quarter, etc. For example what happens if the team produced the following results?

> January – 8.6
> February – 8.8
> March - 9.2

We like this trend! It is moving in the right direction! Of course we want to know why we are improving so we dig into the KPIs to see which categories and which sub categories are improving. We may find out that we are seeing significant improvement in some categories and we are slipping in others. This allows us to congratulate the team on the positive results and refocus our efforts on the areas that need improvement. I heard a great saying early in my career – **You can expect what you inspect**. So true! **KPIs help you achieve that goal.**

To keep it manageable, **I would go to each manager** in the organization and **identify what their team specifically needs to do** – and will do - to achieve their goals. Each team's KPIs may be a little different. Some KPI lists may take a deeper dive than what's on your organization's key performance indicators. That's because the organizations KPI is something everybody looks at so everyone can tell if we are heading in the right direction.

It's also important to set the **KPI tracking** for the entire organization in the same way. Then you drill down into each team and each person to identify specifically what they do and what are their goals. In effect, you are creating key performance indicators for each person in the organization.

Obviously, the KPIs for individuals will be different for teams, supervisors and the entire organization. **The trick is to identify the key activities and categories that really make the most difference.** Once those are identified then it becomes much easier to drive the organization to those selected KPIs that define what "winning" means for the organization.

Of course, there are always other functions that people perform. But if trying to include those activities in the KPIs makes the categories exceed 10 or 12, just ignore them and let the team members know that all these other things are simply expected of all of us. Stuff comes up we all have to do but the KPIs keep each team member focused on what makes their team and this organization a success.

All those individual, team, management and organizational KPIs get rolled up and summarized for the entire organization. That way everyone in the organization is looking at the major KPIs for the company; whether it's the supervisor or the line employee.

In other words, an individual's KPIs obviously may not get much light of day in front of the entire organization. The exception to this is when a particular employee's KPIs are outstanding. Then, it is very important to acknowledge that employee as one of the best performers on the team.

Never forget, working hard is great but acknowledging winning and celebrating success is a crucial part of keeping morale and momentum high. Glossing over an employee's success is one of the quickest ways to stick a pin in the organizational enthusiasm bubble! Don't let that happen – celebrate your successes! Celebrate them often!

Candidly, that's **the other great thing about KPIs; you can use them to identify who are the stellar performers in the organization.**

Instead of some kind of annual Chairman's club or President's club, once a month pick the top five employees in the organization that had the best KPIs scores. Let that be a qualification for them to belong to the President's club or whatever you want to call it. Do the same for each quarter and for the year. It will soon become an exclusive club with top performing employees across the entire organization.

When I did that in Michigan I called it the Coaches Club because I was the "head coach." We would take the top five employees across the state to our regional office once a month.

> *The group would spend the day telling us what they are doing so we could learn from them. We'd take them to lunch and give them a plaque which would recognize and record their accomplishment.*

That's the kind of stuff you can do with it.

Bill's approach to measuring performance with his KPIs provides an ongoing road map for both management and staff.

All too often, supervisors and employees are forced to react - sometimes daily - to upper management's changing priorities. Unfortunately in too many organizations, some new daily priority can override longer term priorities. That causes confusion and wasted time. In others, bosses that scream the loudest set the daily priorities! Either situation is unhealthy and inefficient.

Formal KPIs keeps the focus on specific priorities and the "sand from shifting" under the employee's feet. But when the sand does keep shifting, supervisors and staff alike feel like they are being slapped around like a hockey puck.

Bill's KPIs also do a great job of providing a roadmap for employee bonuses and expectations. High performance is crucial to any successful organization, and shifting priorities only dilutes the time and energy resources of its workforce.

Phil's Thoughts

Strength and conditioning programs are an essential part of the game today. Strength and conditioning have always been important but in the early 60's there was a lot of confusion, speculation and misinformation about strength training. The prevailing belief among trainers - and even many doctors - was that weight lifting would make you muscle bound consequently robbing you of the flexibility so necessary for running, throwing and catching balls. So players, especially at the skilled positions, avoided weight lifting like the plague.

But that has all changed. At every level of football today, high school, college and pro, strength and conditioning programs are the hallmark of a successful program.

Strength and conditioning keeps a team strong and their fundamentals sharp, giving them the confidence and ability to perform at an optimal level. As a rule, players who take this type of preparation seriously are your standouts. The fears of yesteryear are long gone as strength and conditioning programs have paid dividends in player performances, endurance and recovery from injury. The league and its players are indebted to strength and conditioning pioneers like Alvin Roy of Baton Rouge, Louisiana. In the 60's and early 70's, Alvin developed a strength and conditioning regimen for football players. He spent 5 years each with three separate teams; Kansas City, Dallas and San Diego. It wasn't a surprise that each went to the Super Bowl during his tenure.

Having the ability to play the game is just not enough. The ability has to be maintained through constant awareness of the importance of conditioning. There is an old story about a Canadian lumberjack who boasted he could down more trees with his axe than anyone. One day he was challenged by a lumberjack from a neighboring town to see who could cut the most trees in a 12 hour period. The contest started early one morning; the hometown guy was chopping away felling tree after tree and periodically he saw the other lumberjack leaving the area for short periods of time. For sure he was going to beat that guy since he did not plan to stop at all. To his surprise when the end of the day came and the number of trees was counted, the guy from the neighboring town had beaten him by a good amount. "How can that be" he asked the challenger, "I saw you leave quite a few times and I never stopped. What were you doing" he asked. The challenger said "I was sharpening my axe".

JACKIE'S PERSPECTIVE

In business, just like in sports, competition keeps everyone raising his or her performance bar. Was there a difference in the conditioning between the St. Louis Cardinals and Dallas Cowboys in the early and mid-1970s, Jackie?

> Yes there was, Bill.
>
> Dallas had a strength and conditioning coach but St. Louis did not have one. Dallas's conditioning coach's job was to do the type of things I mentioned. He had to monitor the team's strengths and make sure it stayed at the highest level possible throughout the season.
>
> At the time, the Cardinals hadn't picked up on it. Back then there just wasn't enough information out there for people to think it was important. Secondly there was no way to know what any other team was doing unless some guy came from that team and joined yours.
>
> The new player might talk about how they did things but then he's got the job of convincing the coaches on his new team (who have never done it that way), that it is something they should be doing.
>
> If some guy comes from Dallas to our team he will not have to work on conditioning as much as he did at Dallas. However it soon became obvious to all teams in the league that a quality strength and conditioning program was critical before and during the season.
>
> **JACKIE'S PERSPECTIVE**

Getting back to key performance indicators, good supervisors and good managers will know the key things that drive their organization. That's where the KPI building blocks must begin.

For example, let's go back to cable and say that I have a number of supervisors under my direction. The first is a customer service supervisor who has 20 customer service reps to cover the phones. Their job is to answer the phone, take new customer acquisition calls as well as tier-2 service problem calls. Let's also say that I have an installation supervisor that manages 10-20 installers. The installer's job is to go out and install our product in the home.

First, I would go to the customer service manager and ask them what's the ideal customer service rep looks like. If they are good and know their game, the customer service manager will be able to tell me specifically what characteristics they are seeking. They might say, for example, that a great customer service representative:

- Will be able to handle a customer's questions and concerns on average no more than 330 seconds.
- Will have the ability to understand the technical problem within 120 seconds and then escalate it to right source.
- Will be able to handle a new install, a new client and get them their right package and set up within 330 seconds.
- Will be able to answer 95% of the phone calls that come in to the call center within 30 seconds.

That's pretty much a standard you can follow.

Next I'd sit down with the installation supervisor and ask the same kind of questions. The installation supervisor might say that a good installer:

- Can do 5 installs a day.
- That each installation will last on average 106 minutes.
- The average install will include 2.2 products which could be made up of video, data and telephone.
- Will leave behind the proper information on the product (e.g. channel line-up card, etc.)
- Will go over the remote control with the customer.

Next I would ask all the stuff that makes a great employee; what are the key characteristics that help move this organization toward what we want to achieve?

If the goal is to grow the organization through new customer increases then one of the KPIs for the customer care reps becomes an average call length of 330 seconds.

See where I am going? You break it down to what are the key things that move the organization toward the greater goal of growing basic customers. That means reducing customer churn which means you have to be really good at answering customer care problems – tier-1 AND tier-2 problems. You simply identify what are the key winning criteria and then create your standards. That way you can hold your teams, supervisors and employees to their KPIs and that's what you measure them against.

Another interesting use of KPIs is with your children. My son Sam has KPIs that we created to track his school and home performance (think chores) on a weekly basis. His weekly allowance is tied to the results of his KPIs. If he performs all of the tasks he gets 100% of his allowance; if he doesn't, he loses money. He has 10 things he needs to accomplish weekly and some items are worth more than others. The great thing is that Sam calculates his own allowance each Friday afternoon. No more drama! He can also get bonuses if he has 3 months of 100% KPIs. Believe me, this works great and helps a young person learn the results of performance at an early age.

Organizations also need to have a mission statement. They need to define overall who and what they are. If you look at the New England Patriots, their mission statement is pretty simple; "do your job!" Or many people say the mission statement for the Oakland Raiders is "just win baby" - and that came directly from Al Davis.

Earlier in this book I identified the Mission Statement I have used for 25 years – it too, is simple:

Take excellent care of your customers.
Take excellent care of each other.
Do what you say you are going to do.
Celebrate all the blessings that come as a result of your successes.

KPIs will help you measure your way to great success and help you realize your mission. If you don't know what is specifically going on in your company you will be in for a rude surprise and will most likely fail as a leader.

You, as the leader, must not shy away from setting high goals. My teammates always expected me to raise the bar any time we faced a challenge. Frankly, I think every leader needs to be a visionary and not be afraid to ask for high standards of excellence and production from their team. Vince Lombardi, coach of the Green Bay Packers in the '60's, had a quote,

> *"The quality of a person's life is directly proportional to their commitment to excellence regardless of their field of endeavor".*

I have seen his words come true in my teammates. We all rose to new levels of quality of life and have stayed high in the years since we achieved great things. One more thought for leaders; I have always believed that our job is to manage and cultivate human imagination.

Sometimes people just need to be told that they can do it. Michael Jordan, former top player for the Chicago Bulls, used to dream about his shots in games and they would come true. Now, of course, practice has a lot to do with great performance, but if you don't see yourself as a winner you won't be a winner!

It all starts with focus and believing that you can be great.

That means you the reader! Believe in great things! You are destined to be great! Don't let anyone tell you otherwise either! Go make it happen! Let your imagination soar and cool things will happen.

Key Take-Aways from Chapter 5

- Make sure you have the foundation. A house cannot stand if it is built on sand. Same can be said for an organization.
- Know your competition. As much as you can.
- Build your KPIs.
- Celebrate your success!
- Bring successful team members together and learn from them.

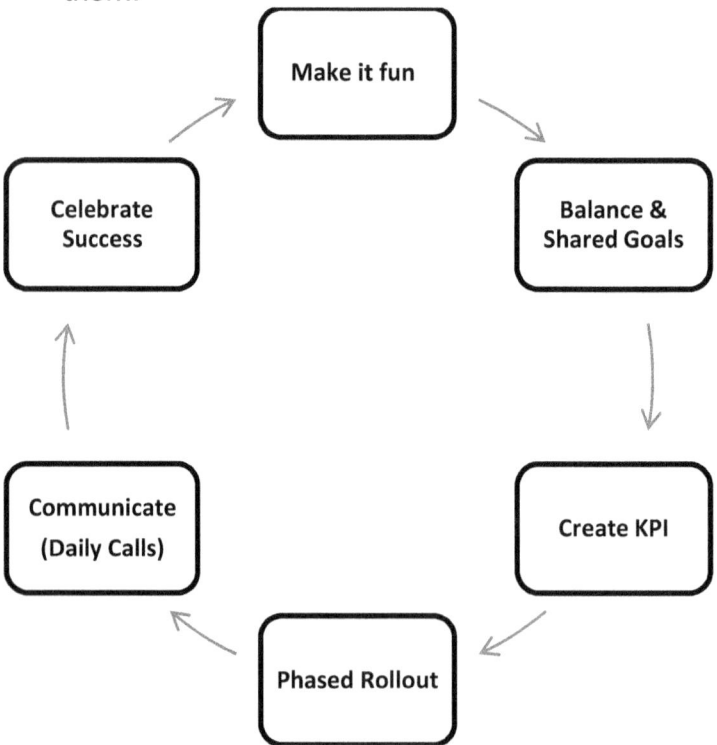

If your organization is not familiar with a results measurement system, it might be too much information to process at once.

Ideas for successful rollout:

- Begin building your KPIs with fewer categories at first
- Add one or two categories each month or quarter
- Begin KPIs without grading until the end of the first quarter they were utilized

Interview with Team Members and Partners

> I learned a lot from Coach Don Shula, who was a stickler for the little things. He used to go crazy over the little things that happened, like making mental mistakes.
>
> His philosophy was if I get on the little things and harp on them, the big things will take care of themselves. When I was with Texo and building my territory, I told Texo I was going to try to get smaller accounts and build a base. Texo sales people were on commission only, so building a base of income was crucial. That strategy was from Shula's focus on taking care of the small things first. Do that first and then build on the base.
>
> Shula also knew every facet of the game. He knew offensive play, quarterback play, line play. He learned to do that from Paul Brown, the legendary coach of the Cleveland Browns, and the founder and first head coach of the Cincinnati Bengals.
>
> One day during a conversation, Coach Shula said to me that if he hired somebody at a position and the guy isn't doing his job, he would have to fill in for that guy. He told me that was why he had to know what is going on in all parts of the game.
>
> That really struck me. As a leader, you just don't learn one facet; you have to learn all parts of the operation. Eventually, something will go wrong so that helps you know what to do. That is basically how I approached things in business - so I wouldn't have to fall back on other people for what I needed to know.
>
> **Bob DeMarco**
> **Past Center, St. Louis Cardinals, Dolphins, Browns, Rams**

Interview with Team Members and Partners

> Bill has a unique way of getting people to work at very high levels, and I think that goes very strongly to Bill's personality.
>
> He's very direct, but at the same time he is your best friend. Bill is there to support you and he makes that very clear. Whatever you need - make the case for it. I don't think Bill ever told me no for anything that I went through and made a detailed and thorough case for what I needed and why.
>
> One other thing Bill did was to instill in us that one person can't make this work by themselves. We just can't do it alone; we can't do it without all the different departments working together. We will succeed together or fail together - but we will not be divided as a team and that made a huge difference.
>
> **Terie Hannay**
> **Past Regional Vice President, Customer Care,**
> **Charter Communications, Michigan**

Interview with Team Members and Partners

> By overlaying that thematic operating process and managing the numbers on a day to day basis, you can react to market and customer conditions on a very rapid basis. That allows the management team to quickly drive change through an organization. It also allows for the betterment of the customers and employees in a much quicker way than I had ever experienced.
>
> This process also allows people to rally people around a singular purpose. That singular purpose is to take care of the customer. When you do that, the business and KPIs generally take care of themselves.
>
> It still shocks me that many industries don't embrace this customer-based process wholeheartedly. Every business has bumps in the road, and no business is not without a down quarter or two from time to time. But by staying focused on the fundamentals of great service and making sure your customers are happy, the KPIs take care of themselves. In the end, the KPIs are just a measurement of how well you are executing your business plan.
>
> It also allows you to get that message out to customers and potential non-customers.
>
> **Jim Holanda, CEO – RCN/Choice Cable**

CHAPTER SIX
EXPANDING THE PLAN
EXECUTING THE PLAN AND MAKING IT WORK...
HALF TIME!

Commitment – it's all about commitment. Whatever you do in life, if you are not committed, then your results will be lackluster.

I've always been competitive in my life in different ways and in different roles. But one of the real turning points came in 1988 when I sat down in my first general manager's chair. That's was really the culmination of everything I ever wanted to do. All of my competitive spirit and juices were flowing, I had the position I knew I wanted and the ability to express myself in a way that really made things tick – it all really brought out my competitive spirit!

That was the first time I was really managing the full spectrum of a business.

I was fully responsible for a $50 million a year business and by the time I left there we had grown to about a $100 million business with over 100,000 subscribers. All of this growth was accomplished over the course of about 6 years.

It was then that I started thinking about all these aspects of the business working together as a team. I also was thinking about how I was going to keep my team tight and enjoying everything. That's when I began to think about how I could create something fun which the team can focus on, everybody can get into and enjoy. One thing led to another and that's when I began to create my thematic motivational ideas.

As I mentioned in an earlier Chapter, my first idea was a yearlong thematic event that I called "Rock N Roll to the 50's." To me, it was about creating an ongoing fun event that became part of our daily working lives. By creating a fun theme, that enthusiasm could flow over and help the team focus on our results while giving ourselves permission to have a good time. We used 50's music, had sock hops to celebrate wins along the way and used this theme for our monthly all employee meeting. It worked very well. We hit our year end goal of 50,000 customers before Thanksgiving!

In fact, it worked so well that our next thematic idea and incentive program was called "Grooving through the 60's." The rationale behind the theme was that now we need to grow to 60,000 customers. We had a lot of fun with that too. The theme laid out what our business goals were and how we were going to do it. Of course, the program included 60's music and everybody dressed like hippies. We had a blast. We also beat our numbers.

All this thematic stuff started the day I sat down behind that desk. I looked down at a blank piece of paper and realized I was responsible; responsible for making sure this organization was a success and that we were going to hit and beat our numbers.

That was when the light bulb came on because I was no longer a member of the supporting cast. Up to that point I was the Regional Controller; somebody that helped put the budgets together and worked with the teams. My job had been to help them with their businesses financial goals but now I was in the hot seat. I was the person who had to pull marketing, customer service, technical operations and finance together. It was my job to get all these different organizations to hit the goals.

That's when it became crystal clear to me I needed something to make the team come together and at the same time to make it fun. In the end, the goal was that we needed to hit our goals. When we did that, we would all get our bonuses, which would then be terrific for ourselves and our families.

Fortunately, even though I was a financial guy I was always a good operations guy.

Obviously I had an accounting degree and understood budgets and finance. But I was "just the bean-counter" and chief financial officer for the region. It was really hard for me to listen to general managers and then be the "No guy", and to say, "No you can't do this", or "No you can't do that!"

More responsibility always breeds more responsibility! I felt an enormous responsibility not just for myself and my family but for everything I did with my team and the company.
I also recognized that my responsibility didn't stop there, but also included my team's families as well. I knew their families, I knew their kids. From the first day in my position as GM, I always felt this tremendous responsibility of making sure we hit our numbers. By meeting or beating our numbers, the whole team would be a real success.

When that happened, everyone on the team and their families could celebrate. We all could enjoy and share in the accomplishments of our achievements. The quality of their lives would improve and they would reap the financial rewards. Remember Coach Lombardi's quote in an earlier chapter. His words were so true! In the end, when we hit and surpassed our goals in a real and honest way, there would never be a question of who would be the highest performing organization within the company. That was always my goal from day one. I wanted to be number one in the company and in everything we did.

Once I put my thematic business development programs into practice, great things started to happen. More and more people in the company wanted to come to work in our cable system. It's funny but my cable system served all of Will County in the Chicago suburbs. It quickly became obvious that 'Will County' took on another meaning. We were the operation that 'will' get the job done.

It was hard to believe the number of employees in the other regions that wanted to work in my system. It seemed as though everyone wanted to be on my team. They looked at Will County and said, "That's where I want to be!"

Honestly, it was because of our team spirit and the incentives we put in place. Everybody knew what they were supposed to do. Nobody had any questions. Every day when they came to work, no one was unclear about what they were supposed to do today - everybody knew what they had to do.

As a result it created an environment where people loved to come to work. Whenever I got up in front of my management teams, the first thing I always said was, "If you want to be successful in your life and business, you have to make the work place a place where people want to come to work".

Most people want to get up in the morning, be enthusiastic about going to work, give it all they've got and then go home at night feeling like they achieved something. If you can do that you are going to be head and shoulders above everybody else.

Some, though, didn't get the memo!

Here's more of a story that we started a few chapters back.

If you will recall, in November 1999, I was hired by Charter Communications to go up to Michigan and build the Michigan region from scratch. Previously, Charter did not have any customers in Michigan but they had recently completed five acquisitions. Charter hired me to be the Regional VP to put together a plan combining these five acquisitions.

In short order, the Michigan region would go from no customers to over 625,000 in just a few months. I went up there in November of 1999 and started working on a budget without any information and didn't have a clue as to what these organizations were going to look like. Neither did we know who these people were or what their past budgets looked like. Yet, the corporate office said we needed a budget for the year 2000 because we have told our investors we are going to hit these numbers. My job, I was told, was to "come down here and tell us all what you are going to do!"

Oh joy!

As you read in the introduction, in late December of 1999 I was instructed to come to St. Louis to attend a 2000 budget review meeting, which turned out to be an incredible fiasco. It was made up of my boss, Dave Barford, the COO and Jerry Kent, CEO of Charter in addition to a lot of the functional heads from the corporate office.

Jerry asked me a ton of questions as we were going through the budgets. My problem was that I didn't have a clue about how all this would come together. For me, doing budgets was kids play, but I really didn't have any hard data to develop the budget and I was scrambling. Jerry later would say that when he thought of that meeting he was "less than impressed". Not a great start for my career at Charter!

Ok, this is where we left off in the story…

So here I am back in Michigan. I'm a financial guy and I know how to put budgets together. Three weeks later there is a quarterly meeting of regional vice presidents in St. Louis. There were 12 of us running the regions then.

Before the meeting one of the RVP's pulled me aside and said, "Bill, whatever you do don't look Jerry in the eyes because his eyes will melt you in your seat. He's like a shark, he'll kill you. Don't make eye contact with him."

So I'm hearing this stuff, my head is crazy and I'm thinking this is going to be nuts.

Jerry begins by going around the room and one by one he asks each RVP if they are going to hit their 2000 annual budget numbers. As he makes his way around the room, the RVP's are waffling and giving Jerry some semi-answers. "I think." "I may." "I'm hoping I can."

Jerry is getting more and more agitated.

He comes around the corner of the table and then it is my turn. Remember, my last encounter with him was a disaster!

I happen to be sitting where I can't directly see him and he says, "Bill what about the Michigan region?"

I leaned forward, looked at him and said, "We will hit our numbers, sir." I leaned back and that is all I said in the meeting.

When the meeting is over, Dave Barford is again driving me to the airport. The quiet was defining but when Dave finally spoke he said in a solemn voice, "You just committed to hit your numbers and Jerry will hold you to it. He said "I wish you the best but make sure you hit your numbers."

Obviously, my counterparts were not happy with me but our "football team" theme was working and the Michigan region was coming on stronger and stronger. As the 2000 year end approached we exploded and blew all the other regions away. They thought it was a joke; they made fun of me and made fun of my team. But by the end of the year they weren't laughing or dissing us anymore.

At the end of year regional meeting, Jerry once again went around the room and was talking about how everybody did on their numbers. When he got to me he stopped and asked me to stand up. When I did, he stood up, then slowly everyone else stood up and they gave me a standing ovation. Jerry said that was the best operational success he had ever seen.

Once again, some people just don't get the memo and you feel like you are fighting up stream. Your counterparts will think you are crazy, people will look at you like you are nuts, but if you get a kernel of an idea put it in place and make it work, it just proves it can happen. You've just got to believe, execute well and make it happen... and don't forget to celebrate along the way.

To refresh you on the Michigan Blizzard plan, we started off 2000 with the "press conference." It was our own internal press conference but we had a lot of fun and everyone needed to stay in character.

Everyone had a jersey and we gave them positions. GM's became quarterbacks, marketers were running backs, customer care people were wide receivers and the field people were both offensive and defensive people.

When we came up to half time in 2000, I rented out the Northern Michigan University Superior Dome in the Upper Peninsula! But all this was a big secret.

That morning before going to the dome, I had school buses pick us up at the hotel. The school buses brought us to the parking lot of the dome and nobody knew what was going on. When we got off the buses, I had a marching band there to greet us. The marching band and I led the team into the dome.

We went into the dome and walked into the locker room and in the locker room was a brand new Jersey for each of the team members. Up to that point, the team had dark jerseys. These new jerseys were white so I told the team that they had won the right to have home field advantage in the 2nd half of the "season." I told them to put on their home jerseys and stand in line.

There they stood, in the tunnel at the very entrance of the dome, while I went out and stood in the center. On cue, the stadium dome lights were killed and a DVD of crowd noise and cheers filled the stadium. We also played Van Halen's song "Jump" to get everyone pumped up!

One at a time I called their name, using the public address system and they came running out of the tunnel.

I had Jerry Kent, CEO, Dave Barford our COO and all the corporate staff waiting on the field with me to high-five everybody as they came through the tunnel. Everyone went wild!

After that Bo Schembechler, the incredible former University of Michigan Wolverines football coach talked for about 45 minutes about leadership and what he did at the University of Michigan. After his rousing talk he signed autographs for everyone.

We then went into an auditorium inside the stadium and had each region put together a video of what the first half of the year meant to them. We also asked them to do a second video about what the second half of the year would mean to them as well.

We showed the videos which were a big hit. With the corporate executives in the audience, I got up on stage; there was a big map of the United States and I had this long poker.

I looked Jerry in the eyes and said, "Jerry, I want you to remember from this day forward, there is one state you don't need to worry about - you don't need to think about - because you know it is going to happen." I pointed to Michigan and my team went crazy.

After that we went back on the field and played football for a couple hours and then worked some more on how we were going to finish strong in the second half. I showed a video that I had made with the voice of the NFL from NFL films. I had a friend in Wisconsin who knows him very well so he did the voice over and talked about the Michigan Blizzard.

In the video, we talked about the first half and then went into the locker room with this cool camera angle. There was a big sign on the door that said **"No score is as unimportant as the score at half time"**.

I started the meeting by telling everybody, "Alright, you had a great first half, but it ain't over. The competition is coming after us and they want to get us in the 2nd half. We have to really be ready! Let's re-set our gameplan for the 2nd half of the year!"

For the next few hours we talked about our gameplans for the 2nd half of the year. We talked about what we needed to do to blow away our numbers by the end of the budget year.

As everyone was filing out of the stadium and getting back on the busses, people were coming up saying it was one of, if not the best day of their lives. They loved this company and it was just unbelievable. We had a fun party that evening where we all discussed the wonderful day each of us had.

The next year we did it even better

The following year the program was pretty much the same as the first year because it went so well. Of course, we tweaked the plan and made it better. Nevertheless, we still had our detractors and naysayers. They just didn't believe that we could have topped our results, but we did! Here is the interesting part – we did it with a new region! We were so successful building the Michigan region that I was promoted to SVP and moved to St. Louis to run the Central Region aka the "mother ship" or the cable system where all of the headquarters folks live, including Jerry. When I got there in March of 2001 the region was forecasting a loss of $1.5 million against their budget. We immediately launched the Central Cyclone football team and ended up beating the 2001 budgeted cash flow by over $3.5 million. That was a $5 million turnaround in 9 months. Believe me, when we won the year and were the best region in the company we had a great celebration.

Once again, we started off with the "press conference." It was our own internal press conference but we had a lot of fun and everyone needed to stay in character.

Everyone had a jersey and we gave them positions. GM's became quarterbacks, marketers were running backs, customer care people were wide receivers and the field people were both offensive and defensive people.

When we came up to half time in 2001, I rented out the Family Arena in St. Charles, Missouri. Again all this was a big secret. When we were number one in the company at the end of 2001 I rented out America's Center in downtown St. Louis and again we celebrated with over 1,200 teammates and their families. What a blast!

Key Take-Aways from Chapter 6

- Pick a theme and go with it! Be courageous. Do something you enjoy. Don't pick boxing (one person sport!).
- Help your teammates want to come to work and be successful. That's a win.
- Believe in yourself and your team. Execute on your plan and make it happen!
- Celebrate! Go ahead and celebrate! In a big way!

Interviews with Team Members and Partners

Bill's thematic approach with KPIs and the daily call keeps people very focused on the things that matter. As a manager when you do that, you don't have a lot of the typical backstabbing and bickering that exists in every organization. You also spend much less time managing HR issues because people are aligned.

It was easy to be comfortable with the process from day-one only because I saw how much success Bill had with his team, and how his team had embraced it in Michigan. With that experience, I knew it was a winning formula. However, I just didn't know how big you could win! Quite frankly it was amazing how much the individuals and team could achieve when "everyone is playing their position." But it happened because day in and day out, everyone played their position to the very best of their ability.

That's what we did with those AT&T properties in 18 months – and no one had probably ever seen that done before in the industry. I think that is a real sense of pride and accomplishment for everyone. We accomplished it all by keeping in mind the fundamental long term best outlook for the customer. That's how we did it.

Jim Holanda, CEO – RCN/Choice Cable

Interviews with Team Members and Partners

I went to work in St. Louis for an old line real estate firm in Clayton called Carl G. Stiffel and Company. I sold houses, did commercial work, office leasing and industrial leasing and I was trying to get some experience. It was common for us back in the 1960s to work at regular jobs in the off-season.

When the Falcons expanded in Atlanta I was picked for that team. Atlanta was exploding in the middle 1960's. I did the same thing there and was able to connect with some really bright people. I learned a new phase of real estate, commercial business and outdoor advertising business.

Eventually we developed 12 patents, built a 15 story residential condominium building and neighborhood shopping centers. We were always looking for opportunities, and not restricted by any fear of trying something new.

One of the important lessons in life that I learned from my Daddy and Coach Dodd was that there aren't any hours specified in a job description. You work until the job is done.

Taz Anderson
Past All American Fullback at Georgia Tech, Tight end St. Louis Cardinals and the Atlanta Falcons

Interviews with Team Members and Partners

> Bill also taught us about celebrating our successes.
>
> While we had those two huge celebrations, most of the time we had smaller celebrations that accompanied our challenges. In my customer care organization, we had lunches and pizza parties. At other times, Bill would have a get-together at the regional office - even if it was a team lunch. We did small things that were intended to celebrate our efforts.
>
> **Terie Hannay**
> **Past Regional Director, Customer Care, Charter Communications, Michigan**

> After the kickoff in March/April, people knew there were going to be KPIs.
>
> So from March to June, people worked on understanding their metrics and began making changes. Most really began to delve a level or two deeper into their organizations. In our case, we discovered that because of the high call volume and thin staff, our customer care people were moving on, too quickly, to the next call.
>
> That meant we couldn't be selling, just answering questions. It didn't take long for us to finally develop the reports. When we did, I said "Wow, I have to hire 20 people like yesterday!" And we did - with awfully quick training - but to have the call center help sell, you have to answer the phone in a timely and friendly manner!
>
> **Terie Hannay**
> **Past Regional Vice President, Customer Care, Charter Communications, Michigan**

Interviews with Team Members and Partners

And then there was the half time celebration! Oh my goodness!

That was the first week of August! We all got on this bus and the ride was very cool.

I would say it was one of the coolest trips our people had ever taken for a business meeting – and to celebrate their success! It wasn't putting on a suit and going in a boardroom and sitting with your peers for 6 hours and getting bored to tears. It was a working meeting but a celebration at the same time. It was an exciting but productive open discussion. Again, you have a group where the walls have been torn down; we are all working together and people aren't hiding their problems.

Originally, Bill developed what he called "stretch goals", which soon became our real goals. Right after the kickoff meeting we were all in a room and identified what we had to do to hit the budget. But at the half time event, the stretch goals became the actual goals. It's when we pulled together a plan to do hit and beat our numbers.

That's when everyone's expectations changed, too. It was fine and people were ready for that increased challenge. But at the beginning, if Bill would have told us that those numbers were our real goals, he would have lost some people. I'm not sure they would have grasped that they could do it at the time.

But that caused us to focus more critically on what we were doing. We drilled further into each call - turning a question into a sale. We improved how we answered the phones and how to offer additional services. Sales took-off after that. We went from just answering the phones, to making sure the customer was happy at the end of the call. We also measured and incentivized the results through our KPIs.

Oh yea, at the event, Bo Schembechler was the guest speaker and he was really something.

Terie Hannay
Past Regional Director, Customer Care, Charter Communications, Michigan

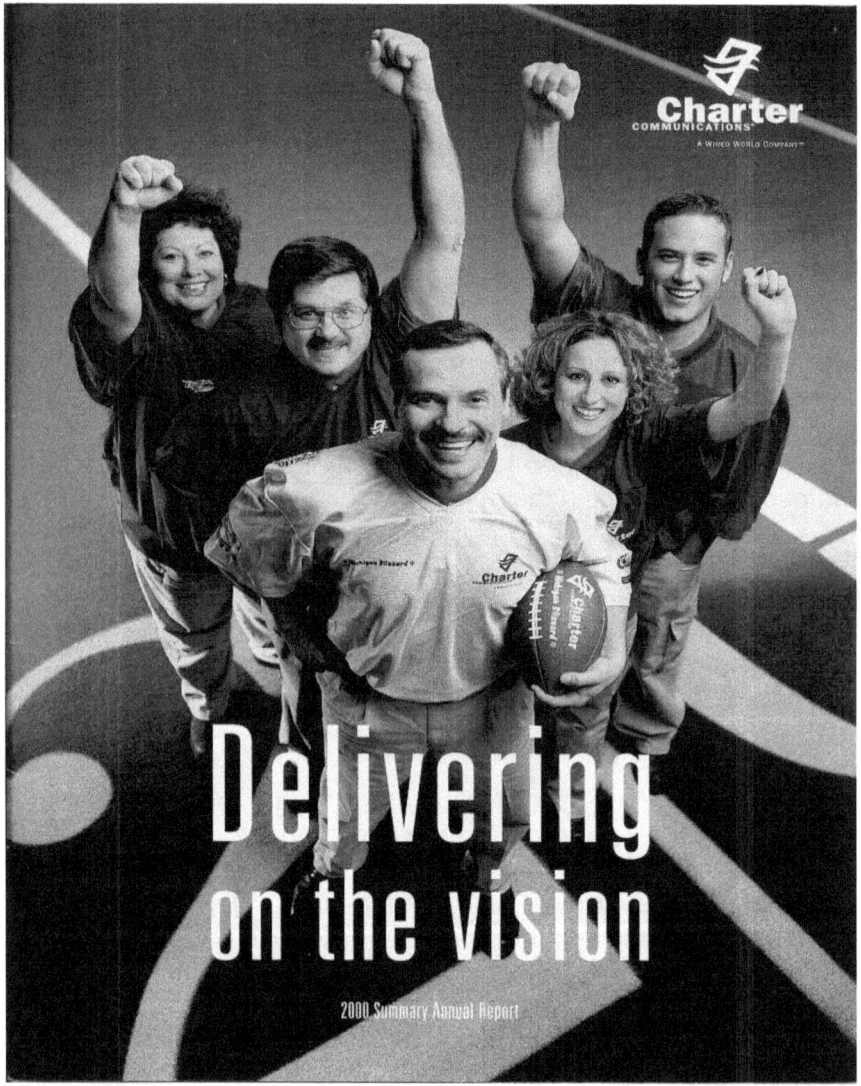
The Michigan Blizzard on the cover of the 2000 Charter Communications Annual Report

Band meets the Blizzard management team at the Half Time event held at Northern Michigan University Superior Dome

Blizzard team marches with the band into the stadium

New jersey's to signify our home team colors

Terie Hannay runs out of the tunnel

Bo Schembechler addresses the Blizzard team

Reviewing our Gameplan for the second half

Everyone on the Blizzard management team had an 'on field' picture opportunity

The Cyclone management team at the Family Arena for the Half Time event

Coach Bill addressing the Cyclone team

Cyclone management team picture

Bill and members of the senior team rockin' at the Year end celebration

The Champions arrive at Michigan State University for the Half Time event

Coach Bill addresses the Champion management team

Jackie Smith delivering his thoughts to the Champion team

Reviewing our Gameplan for the second half

Jackie and Bill at Half Time

Bill's Blizzard and Cyclone Championship Rings

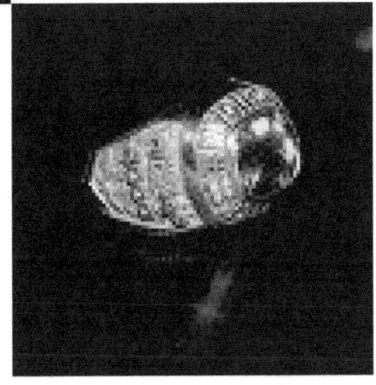

CHAPTER SEVEN
BECAUSE HE SAID TO – HE'S THE COACH....
STAYING FOCUSED

When people hear about what we did in Michigan, I'm often asked, "How did you get everyone to play along with your football scheme... I mean theme!"

I liked the way my executive assistant, Dee Porter, answered the question. Occasionally someone asked Dee, "Why are we doing this?" She was a terrific sounding board for the employees and had a special way about her. Here is what she often said when asked that question:

I think initially a lot of people were skeptical because, of course, they had never experienced anything like this before. Until then, work was work; it was mostly boring. You came in, did your job and went home.

When Bill arrived on the scene it kind of shook everybody up. Initially they were thinking what the heck? But as the employees saw other employees doing what Bill was trying to get everybody to do; they quickly picked up on it. Once they joined in they thought, "Wow, now we're having fun".

I have never worked anywhere where we did anything like this - not even remotely close to this. So the initial thought was maybe he's a little wacko - whoever heard of doing this. But it didn't take long.

Within a month, pretty much everybody was on board. If you weren't, it honestly wasn't fun. If you didn't participate - if you didn't believe that it could be fun – you'd be miserable. Everybody else was having fun, believing and knowing this is the goal and we are going to reach it. We were just going to do it.

At the beginning some were sitting on the sidelines thinking, "This is crazy; this is crap, that can't be fun." But that usually didn't last long. I think most people became believers by watching their co-workers dive in and enjoy the water.

No one ever gave me specific negative comments. But, when some would ask "why are we doing this?" my answer was always the same, "because he said to. Bill's the coach, he said to do it and he knows what he's talking about. If you do it, it's going to work." But every once in a while there were a few that would question what Bill was doing.

Dee Speaks

When we were at Broadstripe we had a region that was not performing very well at all. We could tell that from our daily call. This region was lagging behind and wasn't hitting their KPIs. It quickly became apparent that something was wrong and it was only getting worse.

As I often did, I sent one of our key team members out there to see what was going on - you know, feet on the ground. When the person I sent reported back, the reasons were crystal clear.

The local ops manager had personally named his team – he assigned people instead of using our staffing approach. He did not ask his team for feedback and didn't make achieving their goals a fun thing. He ignored our football theme, never handed out jerseys and never did anything that the other successful groups were doing. The successful regions were fully engaged in our football approach and having fun. As a result his region was way off its numbers and as it turned out, was the only region that did not embrace our methodology. Yep, you guessed it. I did the football theme again at my new company Broadstripe. We called the team the Champions.

Needless to say, we corrected the problem immediately. That particular manager ended up pursuing a job as a trainee in the "food services industry", my phrase for saying someone has moved on to their real calling.

As C-suite executives, we really need to make sure that managers and leaders in the organization have the right priorities. That includes caring about the people you manage and all of your co-workers, not just your family. That's not something you can fake for very long. People recognize a fake very quickly and then you are dead in the water.

Here's a story that I think will illustrate the point. It was the early 1990s and I was a general manager with Continental Cablevision running Will County.

We just got through our Rock 'n Roll with the 50's and hit all our numbers. By the time we shifted into 2nd gear, (the next year), we were Groovin' to the 60s, hitting all our numbers – AGAIN. Everybody in the region wanted to work in my system.

I pointed out in the last chapter that what people could see from the outside was that our team was having a blast and beating our numbers. Everybody wants to be a winner and our colleagues in other parts of the region wanted to be part of what we were doing.

I will never forget, we were in a regional retreat and my boss came up to me at the end of the day when we were unwinding. My team and I were sitting at the bar or playing pool, all of us having a good time together. We did things like that together often. But today, there are some things you really can't do anymore, like this: sometimes on Friday nights when the techs would come back from their work for the day, we would have two big kegs of beer which we would tap right there in the parking lot. We would have bands playing music and we would unwind, tell stories and just talk until about midnight.

Needless to say, we really had a tight team.

Sometime later at the regional retreat, my boss came up to me and said, "How do you guys do this? How have you pulled this stuff together?"

At the same time my counterparts all crowded around me. I began with a comment, which too, came out of nowhere. I looked around at my team and said, "I'm the king of the s%#! house rats. Most of the management looked at us like we were some weird stepchild. They thought we were going to be way off the reservation and nobody thought that we could do what we've done. But at the end of the day we pulled it off.

We have a great team and everybody on the team knows what they need to do."

My boss kind of muttered a few things, complimented us and I didn't give it another thought.

At our next monthly all-employee meeting something different happened. These meetings would last about 45 minutes. We'd talk about where we were relative to our goals, awarded our Employee of the Month plaque and any other important items that were appropriate for our meeting.

About halfway through the meeting my boss shows up – the one that came up to us at the regional meeting. That was normal because every once in a while he would poke his head in to say hi and listen to what we were doing. Then HIS boss, the Senior Vice President of the entire area in Chicago, shows up! I'm thinking this is going to be kind of strange because he doesn't normally come to any of our meetings. But, he's a good guy and I'm ok with it.

All a sudden, one of my managers says, "Bill, stop right there. We have a ceremony we want to go through." I said, "A ceremony?" He said, "Yes, we have to officially award you the King. So they gave me a T-shirt with the words 'King of the S%#! House Rats' emblazoned on the front! They made me put it on right there.

Then all my teammates put on their 'S%#! House Rats' T-shirts. They gave my boss a 'King of the King of the S%#! House Rats' T-shirt and his boss - the big cheese SVP came up to the front of the meeting and they gave him the 'King of the King of the King of the S%#! House Rats' T-shirt. We all laughed and kidded until the meeting ended. What a blast!

I'm telling you this because this episode is one of those events that may sound cheesy, it may sound goofy, but it is one of those things that people embrace and they enjoyed.

The fact that I referred to them as the S%#! House Rats didn't matter a bit. They were all part of the team and really appreciated the humor. The other people outside my team could call us whatever they wanted. We got the job done, blew away our numbers and had a great time doing it. On a relative basis, we blew right by the other regions and never looked back.

Remember the movie the Dirty Dozen? These people were in the trenches, but they knew how to get it done and they did not care what other people thought. That was our attitude: you can call us whatever you want but we are going to beat our numbers and make it happen.

Here's a follow up to that story. When I left Continental in 1995, you would have thought I was leaving for the moon. There must have been four going away parties. It was like a wake and everybody was asking if I really had to go. Two or three months after I left I kept getting phone calls from the team. I was in Colorado and then I ended up going to Australia for a month. Even in Australia they were calling to give me a hard time!

So it is one of those things to be careful for what you ask! Obviously, it was a really good feeling to be needed and know the team was that tight. It was pretty cool. By the way, that team was family to me. I cared about all of them.

That is really about the highest compliment you could've gotten, Bill. You created a great atmosphere that was filled with execution, attention to detail, fun and winning. That's a great combination.

Obviously football has a certain atmosphere and the players and coaches want to be a part of it. But to stay in that atmosphere, players had to execute – they knew what was expected. We have a lot of fun there too, because you are able to communicate in a different way with guys, kidding them or setting them up to do something or whatever.

But what you've done is to make what is usually a mundane business thing and put together something that is a lot of fun for everybody. You have given them a purpose and set the atmosphere for having fun. More importantly, letting people know it is okay to have fun - it is okay to laugh.

At the same time you're getting some pretty serious stuff done. It's a hell of a combination that you created where people could have so much fun with the concept. The way you set things up your team didn't have to think about it. The KPIs were to us like 1st downs, 3rd down conversions and red-zone executions.

JACKIE'S PERSPECTIVE

> It was something that was natural, a lot of fun and it was really a great atmosphere that you created. When that happens, people enjoy it so much that they want more and more of it. They look aggressively to find more ways to have fun with it and be more creative. It all feeds on itself. To me, it is very interesting to hear all that happened while you were putting all the pieces together.
>
> **JACKIE'S PERSPECTIVE**

Thanks Jackie. But as I was saying earlier in this chapter, it's all about integrity; integrity of the organization, integrity within the organization and the integrity of each employee. If integrity doesn't permeate every pore of the organization, everything can fall apart in a heartbeat.

When you look in the mirror, you must be able to know, without a doubt, that you care about the organization, each employee in the organization and every customer that the organization serves. It's not just about your job and the company goals. It's that you deeply care about the people you work with - I mean really care about them!

Sure, you can care about the business and its goals and objectives but if you don't care about your team, you are dead in the water. You might as well just do something else with your life. As Jackie pointed out, people will recognize a fake very quickly. You might try to fake it for a while but before long, the employees will know when you don't believe something and then you have lost all credibility.

So in the end, if you really don't care about the company, the employees and the customers, you're not going to go anywhere. If that's the case, maybe you need to find a job as a trainee in the 'food services industry'!

> That is really true, people don't really care about how much you know until they can find out how much you care about them.
>
> **JACKIE'S PERSPECTIVE**

Key Take-Aways from Chapter 7

- Get **all** of your teammates on board with your plan.
- Keep "A" players and send the "B" and "C" players back to the practice field for more training.
- Care about your teammates….really care.
- Don't forget to laugh at yourself and have fun.
- Have integrity always.

Interview with Team Members and Partners

> As far as being part of the team, you didn't necessarily have to like the player you were playing with. But if he was a good player, you'd adjusted to it; we have a common cause and go ahead and do it. That helped out a lot in business because a lot of people we called on we didn't always like personally, but you found a way to work with them.
>
> Again, responsibility, discipline and passion for something are what you basically carry over from football into a business.
>
> **Bob DeMarco**
> **Past Center, St. Louis Cardinals, Dolphins, Browns, Rams**

> I was somewhat on the outside looking in at the success Bill was generating for 2 years in Michigan using his program. But within 6 months, I was a huge believer. I always knew I would use it in whatever my first true operations or leadership opportunity would be.
>
> I was very fortunate to have the opportunity to work for Bill, and to watch and participate in his thematic process. Through that process, I was able to embrace it wholeheartedly. Bill is a great coach, mentor and role model. I clearly wouldn't have been able to execute it as well as I did if I didn't have Bill's daily guidance.
>
> **Jim Holanda, CEO – RCN/Cable Choice**

CHAPTER EIGHT
HALFTIME AND THE TRANSITION INTO THE THIRD QUARTER

> **The Mission Statement**
>
> *Take care of the customer,*
> *Take care of each other,*
> *Do what you say you're going to do,*

and... **Celebrate the blessings along the way** - halftime is in an unbelievable opportunity to celebrate.

We celebrated our initial achievements and made sure that everyone understood how important their daily efforts and attention to detail really was for the team.

Our halftime celebrations included some incredible events and many were once-in-a-lifetime opportunities.

Here we were in Michigan, we're coming up on June and we're coming up on the results for what we did in Q2 2000. Clearly, the team was really starting to move the ball. We are growing customers, are ahead of our budget and things are moving in the right direction. As the head coach I called halftime for early August, I think it was August 3rd through August 6th.

The message to business is that halftime does not have to be July 1 or June 30. It can be anytime you want to call halftime. That choice is up to you and you are the coach.

We identified that at halftime we go to the locker room; we revisit the first half, get pro-active for the second half and keep the momentum going. While we really did celebrate first half successes, we were always mindful of it "ain't over till it's over."

Remember the big sign on the door:

> **"No score is as unimportant as the score at half time"**

Those are the kind of key over-arching principles we talked about during the year.

As we went along through the first half the year, we had fun with it. We'd kid around and say that if we didn't hit our numbers by halftime we were going to stay in some downtown hotel in Detroit with no air conditioning, it was going to be about 105° in the rooms and we were going to spend 2-3 days going line by line through the budget.

Or - if you beat your budgets we will give you an opportunity you will never forget. So everybody took us up on that offer and said they wanted to see something that they would never forget!

But once the halftime celebration is over, half time adjustments begin. This process is a more focused assessment of how the overall "game" is going. It's an opportunity to make adjustments, tweak plays and in some cases, make significant adjustments when something new or unexpected, changes the shape of the game.

All too often, managers and executives become very driven and forget about having fun. But if you care about your teammates – your employees – it's important to stop and smell the roses.

Managers that habitually don't have fun and are all work can quickly wear-down their employees. Employees are not machines and it's critical to always keep that in mind. That said, each manager has his or her own style. But in the end, if the manager can't find the way to relieve the stress and tension and make it fun, then something has to give. All too often, employees simply think you don't care about them and that the company looks at them as just a machine. If you aren't good at having fun, find someone in your organization that is good at it and make them the "fun" leader.

That kind of attitude really comes through. The trick is to find a way to connect with your people and incorporate a specific and intense way of having fun. If you can't do that then what often develops is that you quickly leave bodies along the trodden path.

That is what instituting a program like our football team allows you to do. It gives you the opportunity to use football terms and analogies. It allows you to figure out how to have that fun. How? Because by wearing the jersey, you get into a role, it's almost like you are an actor. You bring others into the process and the child-like quality begins to blossom into something fun and effective. Heck, even when I was the Chairman, President and CEO of Broadstripe we wore our jerseys at every quarterly board meeting. In fact, all of our board members wore their jerseys. They had a blast wearing them to the meeting.

In fact, I believe one of the most important things that can happen to a leader is to never let go of that childlike view of the world. It often pays to see the world with fresh eyes.

As the old adage goes, "Growing old is mandatory, growing up is optional." This allows you to role play and have some fun, dress-up and do some goofy stuff that you never thought you would want to do as an adult. But once you do, it puts you in a whole different mood and a whole different mode. It sets the platform for having fun. Remember earlier I said that it is the leader's job to manage human imagination. Believe and let your team believe. Have fun and let your team have fun.

All this is not just for rank and file employees, but for your management staff, too.

Early in my career, I would devour books on techniques and management philosophies. While reading, I would highlight passages and bring those books into our staff meetings.

At the end of the meetings, I would read some of the key things; one of them was in the book "In Search of Excellence" by Tom Peters. In there was a chapter where I discovered the "loose/tight" management style. That was something that I completely embraced and taught my team.

In business there are certain issues on which you had to remain very "tight" and not waiver. Other less critical issues gave you the flexibility to be "loose", and dial back the intensity. In fact, there are a lot of things in business you can be loose on. But subjects like budgets, hitting your numbers, taking care of each other - all of these critical things - you have to be tight on.

Make sure you take the time to know which are critical and which have some wiggle room. Stay "tight" with those that are critical and be "loose" with the rest. When you do that, employees naturally know what your priorities are. Prioritizing items in this loose / tight strategy can make the day go a lot smoother. Heck we are all living our lives and trying to enjoy the journey. Remember, it's not the destination; it's the journey.

> I think that is a big point.
>
> That's the same thing the coaches do too; they make sure you get the most important things right. The best coaches understand there are a lot of things that aren't that critical and don't need the same type of enthusiasm applied to them.
>
> It makes everything a little fuzzy when you are not quite sure where the coach's head is sometimes. The best coaches tend to the basics and cut you a little slack on some of the others - but not much…
>
> The best coaches are very particular about that and know exactly what is important. They make sure that everybody knows it and leaves it there.
>
> **JACKIE'S PERSPECTIVE**

It's like the whole concept of "dare to be different." Be different, let yourself go and let yourself be creative.

I will never forget what happened at the party we had at the end of the year in Michigan. We had over 1200 employees in Michigan, just had the big dinner and there was not a dry eye in the place. My wife Kristie and I were walking back to our room and an advertising sales representative came running up to me dragging her husband. She said, "I have to tell you Bill I love this company. This was the coolest thing I have ever been to in my life", and she burst out crying. She said "you made me feel like I am somebody, thank you". It was incredible. That is one of those things that you think if I can do this for one person in my lifetime then it is all worth it.

> You are exactly right. I've been through situations like that and that is a life changing experience.
>
> You've made them believe that it is possible, you guide them, they do it and they will never be quite the same again after that.
>
> They will always be looking for that and never satisfied with anything else except that type of motivation, that type of environment that they will be working in.
>
> You spoiled a lot of people Bill!
>
> **JACKIE'S PERSPECTIVE**

Future business football teams I coached had a few slight variations but overall the basic theme was pretty much intact. One thing we did was to bring in a couple of football guys, which is an understatement.

We brought in Bo Schembechler who did a great job up at the UP but I think we improved a bunch when we got Jackie Smith involved. Jackie did a great job of talking to the team. He was somebody that the employees could talk to and learn from. Jackie also became a good friend to the team. He sat at the tables, talked to people, hung out and he partied with us. We all really enjoyed him. Everyone there really got a chance to get to know Jackie and made him a part of their team. It was such fun!

If you look at the group, several things changed. In addition to their commitment, there was awareness for the first time in what they could accomplish. It's almost like you took the blinders off.

For the first time, leaders were able to look at their organizations in a different way. They were able to stand up and say, I did these things well. Or, if they didn't do so well they would say this is what I'm going to do to improve in the second half. You could actually see people learn how to be better leaders, better planners and better motivators. It was just a natural kind of environment where people were able to spread their wings.

On top of that the other great thing I saw was the esprit de corps where the team just got so tight together. We had been on the phone everyday together, we won these battles together, we partied together and we went to the Stadium together.

You could just see how it really broke down the barriers that are the norm in a lot of organizations. Most organizations have lots of "walls" and turf battles; I am 'Sales' and you're 'Accounting'. All of that was just crushed because there was an overall goal. Everyone was focused on the goal. They knew what it meant to win and everybody was doing their part to win. It was a terrific experience.

> Like Bill said, the camaraderie improved tremendously. There wasn't any of the normal my-team against your-team. Everyone was on the same team and if one team could help the other, they would and they were willing to share ideas.
>
> ### *Dee Speaks*

A good example is a guy who was the regional engineer. One time they ran out of converters, which are the boxes the service staff puts in your house. He found out that another region had a bunch of them.

This guy wanted to make sure that we won, so he rented a truck and trailer and drove from Michigan to St. Louis. When he got there, he loaded the converters onto the trailer himself, drove them back up to Michigan, offloaded them and gave the service staff what they needed to get the job done!

Most employees live under shackles. They are always told what they can't do as opposed to what they can do. When you start telling people what they can do and what you expect them to do, that is when people start getting really creative.

Our theme approach proved its worth, not once, not twice but time and again. That's the basic part that I would always do: the parties and the structured meetings.

Of course, there can be variations depending on the team. If it wasn't a football theme but some other type of incentive theme, I would still stop at some point in the year. Call it halftime or call it something else but you need to have a stopping point.

You could even have a different name for it; call it celebration time, intermission or something like that.
But you always have to take the time to talk about the obvious - I know things are tough and I know we have a lot on our plates. But then you need to take a couple days to go back over all the good things that your team has achieved.

We will always need to talk and plan about the things we have ahead of us. But let's take time to celebrate the things that have happened.

Every organization needs to do some celebrating otherwise life can quickly become a grind. You can grind people into the dirt, keep piling on more and more, but eventually people will say, "Hey, what's the deal? You're killing me!"

This is what I talked about at the very beginning of the book. The cool thing about doing these types of programs is you can actually make meaningful changes in people's lives. Today is no longer the same as yesterday and it's not the same as tomorrow.

Now people have a goal and they know that there is a specific date for hitting that goal. After that goal there is going to be a new goal, but boy when we hit this goal, we are going to have a party, celebrate and feel good about what we did.

At the celebration you can give away trophies, have fun.

Soon enough you'll have the opportunity to start again. But having a thematic approach helps people get through the process so that the grind of everyday targets doesn't wipe them out. If you don't let your people get ground down they will keep going and be much happier for a long time. Most importantly, you will actually find that their home lives can improve too. They'll be less stressed at the end of the day and even learn how to bring more fun into their personal lives.

What I've found is that in business the norm is to treat today just as yesterday and tomorrow as today. Drive, drive, drive. Grind, grind, grind.

But from my perspective, it's the opposite. To be successful and have a happy and motivated workforce, you can't treat today the same as yesterday.

These types of incentives - these types of management philosophies - break up the daily grind when you have quarterly goals; halftime and you have a year-end celebration.

Here is the key, you must have markers [in time] that identify - I hit this goal. That goal is done. I've achieved that goal and I'm at the top of the mountain. Tomorrow I'm going to go climb to the next mountain. But not without some fun along the way!

> Bill, you also have created so many touchstones as far as the experiences are concerned. That is a lot like athletics as far as practicing for, getting ready and playing the game.
>
> So many things that you are involved in that take your attention and distract you from the goal.
>
> And it's not the same every week. You have a new opponent but the camaraderie and enthusiasm that the team has formed is what will sustain you. The team is trying to win each game and that is what keeps you going, keeps you motivated and keeps it enjoyable.
>
> If it was any other way I just don't think you would get many people wanting to play. It's got to be that emotional involvement, emotional reward on top of the physical part that has to be put into it.
>
> In football you get so many emotional rewards – and emotional touchdowns.
>
> **JACKIE'S PERSPECTIVE**

Exactly to that point, Jackie, how many companies take the opposite track with the motto of the old saying that, "The beatings will continue until morale improves."

It's too bad and all-too-often true but that's the way too many companies are managed.

It's important to recognize that the nature of business is to continually grow and improve profitability. The competitive need for new and improved products and services and the delivery of those products and services to the market place is the hallmark of successful businesses. If you are going to operate and lead a successful business, every executive, manager and supervisor has to continually go back to their employees and motivate them to do more and often with less.

That is where an enjoyable, theme-oriented working environment shows its strength. Our key performance indicators (KPIs) and our daily calls kept all of us on track and focused. Each person knew what they had to get done today and how they had to execute. If they missed their number today or this week they would need to figure out how to make up for the difference next week.

This can be a relentless and grinding process, unless you can find a way to off-load the stress and drudgery. What we proved in all five thematic approaches:

- Rock 'n Roll to the 50s",
- Groovin to the 60s,
- The Michigan Blizzard,
- The Central Cyclone, and
- The Broadstripe Champions

What we proved was that we could raise the relative level of performance of every organization to heights they had never before achieved within those company structures. It was intense, with lots of heavy-lifting, but we found a way to have fun, achieve our goals and celebrate our successes along the way.

What organization wouldn't what to achieve that combination of high-performance, high quality, activity and customer-driven success?

I can't think of one, can you?

Today is the time to step up to the line. Dare to be different! Let yourself go and unlock your creativity…

The third quarter begins… NOW!

Talk about reaching out and touching everyone!

Bill's Daily Call is a masterful approach to solving the ongoing difficulties of clearly communicating with all levels of the organization. From the top and deep into the organization, each listener gets to hear how the other parts of the company are performing against their KPIs. This certainly keeps the focus where it needs to be!

Another unique feature of Bill's Daily Call is that they are usually short and to the point: often just 15 to 30 minutes. While the management team reports, the other listeners get a laser-like version of the ongoing activities. This is peer pressure with a velvet hammer!

Finally, Bill's Daily Call is obviously the conduit for his energetic and thematic management approach. Bill runs 10 miles a day and keeps his own energy high. His daily call is a key method for transmitting that high energy throughout his organization.

Phil's Thoughts

Key Take-Aways from Chapter 8

- "No score is as unimportant as the score at half time".
- Promote fun yourself or get a "fun leader".
- Dare to be different.
- Break down the walls and develop one strong team.
- Stop halfway through the year and take stock of your success (or lack thereof) and plan for the remainder of the year.

Interviews with Team Members

> The high-expectation, open, honest and fun environment that Bill created was key to what we accomplished.
>
> It took the first 6 months of 2000 to get everybody's sea legs and pulling in the same direction. But once we did, sales and profitability took off like a hockey stick - it went straight up. Let me say again, everybody was pulling in the same direction and for the same goal.
>
> The noise that exists in a lot of corporations didn't exist in Bill's region.
>
> Fingers weren't being pointed and no one was saying "I could do this better if so and so would do that better." All of those walls were down. Instead, Bill's attitude that permeated the organization was if someone needs help, we will all work together to solve the problem.
>
> **Terie Hannay**
> **Past Regional Director, Customer Care, Charter Communications, Michigan**

CHAPTER NINE
THIRD QUARTER – IT STARTS AGAIN
THE CONCEPT OF HUSTLE...

In football, the third quarter marks the start of the final half of play. In business, Q3 represents the start of the stretch towards the end of the year. It's an opportunity to apply the lessons learned during the first half and fine-tune what was learned at halftime.

When we came out of our halftime meetings there were several things we talked about and implemented. Of all of them, the concept of Hustle was one of the key points. In fact, we made slides of the bullet points and printed them out so that team members could tape them around their desks and cubicles.

"Hustle" is an important concept. It conveys purposeful energy and motion. Hustle also conveys the enthusiastic intent that a person or organization has for achieving their goal

The first bullet point was hustle. Derric Johnson once wrote the following comments about Hustle and it became one of our war cries:

> **WHAT IS HUSTLE?**
> **HUSTLE IS DOING SOMETHING...**
> **THAT EVERYONE IS ABSOLUTELY**
> **CERTAIN...CAN'T BE DONE.**

This was probably the biggest war cry for the Michigan Blizzard.

Everybody at corporate and virtually everybody in the company thought there is no way we were going to be successful. Everyone "KNEW" Michigan was going to be a disaster! Don't you love consensus? Well, we showed 'em that hustle is doing something everyone is absolutely certain can't be done!

The second bullet point was this:

> HUSTLE IS GETTING THE ORDER
> BECAUSE YOU GOT THERE FIRST…
> OR STAYED WITH IT…
> AFTER EVERYBODY GAVE UP.

Then we talked about intuitiveness.

98% of life is showing up, hanging in there, just keep working it, putting your shoulder to the wheel and keep pushing, pushing and pushing. Oh yea, and don't forget to have lots of fun while you are keeping on - keeping on!

The third bullet point is:

> HUSTLE IS…
> SHOE LEATHER…ELBOW GREASE…
> SWEAT…AND MISSING LUNCH.

I would ask people in the meeting to give me a show of hands who had missed lunch in the last couple of weeks? Everybody would raise their hand because everybody was working hard to try and get their stuff done; they missed lunch, they missed dinners and all kinds of stuff!

The fourth bullet point is:

> HUSTLE IS GETTING PROSPECTS TO SAY
> YES…AFTER THEY SAID NO 20 TIMES.

We used to talk about "no" and that it simply was the journey of getting to yes.

You talk to your clients, you talk to customers and you just continue to understand what their barriers were to the sale. We didn't employ high pressure. Rather, we kept listening and knocking down the objections until we got to the point where the sale COULD be made in a positive and WIN-WIN way.

We kept refining our services until the customer would be able to say, "Okay I will try your system."

The fifth bullet point is:

HUSTLE IS PROVIDING MORE FOR YOUR CUSTOMER...THAN YOUR COMPETITION.

We talked a lot about by providing not only services that others don't have but also providing the highest standards of quality service.

We were all about getting out there for the installation, the service call and all the things that go along with providing great customer care.

It used to drive me crazy when I would ask my managers what customer care is to them. Most would quickly say it's the people in my call center that handle customer calls. While that was the "normal" answer, I always saw it differently. I'd usually say that is part of it, but:
- Customer care begins with the very first customer contact.
- It continues with the installation of the product.
- It is teaching the customer how to use the service.

- Finally, it is listening to what the customer says so we can improve our services in our offices and in the field.

This is how we serviced our customers. By the time a complaint would get to our customer care department, the reality was that we had failed. Something went wrong somewhere and in some way we failed.

If a customer is calling to complain in some way, whether it is about their bill or something about the service, then I wanted to see everything that happened before it got to the call center. That was our audit process, which we continually talked about, too. KPIs – Key Performance Indicators – are simply part of the audit process.

Again, this whole process was designed as a win-win situation. We never condoned any high pressure tactics. Those only backfire. In fact, our training manuals would go into detail on several high touch ways to work with prospects and new customers.

Our goal was for the prospect or customer to WANT to do business with us because our reputation for quality service was a consistent message we tried to put forth. But you can't just advertise the concept of customer service; it has to be backed up every day and on every call.

We went about it a couple ways. The first was either through our direct or telemarketing sales efforts or when a potential customer called one of our call centers.

There were three ways we could actually touch a potential customer.

- On the **direct sales** side, we had our direct sales team give continual training on how to sell to the customer. In fact, from time to time I would actually go out with the direct sales team and go door-to-door. That way, I could hear what the potential customer was saying, to see their response and see what was happening. I would ride in the car, go to the door and be part of the presentation. Afterwards I would debrief the direct sales representative what they did right and what they could have done better.

- On **customer care**, we would give our customer care reps training on how to overcome objections, handle questions and most importantly, how to stay in a very pleasant state. We would actually teach them to smile while they were on the phone. We did that because we learned that the customer can tell you are smiling. If you are grouchy or you have a sour demeanor, it will come through on the phone. So, our training taught the call center rep to practice smiling while they were talking. Smiling "upped" our game and it definitely sounds much more pleasant.

- We also had online **scripts** the reps could use. When a customer asked a certain question, the rep could go to a script on their computer and actually walk the customer through the answer. These scripts greatly helped the reps explain the answer better as well as help the reps overcome objections by being helpful and pleasant.

Telemarketing also had their own scripts. There is no substitute for continual training. If we had a rep that was doing really well, we would make that rep a trainer. We'd have them meet with the head of training and tell the manager what they were doing that was working so well. That was cool because number one, they are doing great and number two, the rep felt good and really contributed to our process. When the rep/trainer got up in front of his or her team, their confidence and pride increased when they could talk about what they were doing that worked so well.

Our call center had a full-time customer care trainer. All the calls were recorded so the trainer would gather together different vignettes. Every customer care rep had to go through every training module. Modules were continually updated, so at least every two or three months, every rep would get recertified. We made training and recertification part of their job description. As the rep took the training they would move up in levels and pay-grades as well. We had a CSR3, CSR2 and a CSR1 and that training was the guideposts to how the reps were promoted and earned more money.

All this training and attention to detail gave us our accelerating momentum when we went into the third quarter and eventually the fourth quarter. We found that through our regiment of training we could integrate new information which was being continually uncovered.

The sixth bullet point is:

HUSTLE IS BELIEVING IN YOURSELF AND THE BUSINESS YOU ARE IN.

I used to tell everybody - if you don't believe:

- That Charter Communications is the best company you could ever work for;
- That it provides the best services that are available in the market;
- Then you need to go find something else to do.

When I was the GM in Chicago in the late 80s to the mid-90s, I used to have what I called *"The $30 Challenge."*

This was in the days before high-speed data or all-digital services and before DirecTV and Dish came along.

Every month I would challenge everybody in my organization - about 150 employees. At all employee monthly meetings, I would get up in front of them and hold up $30 in cash. Then I would say that everybody knows our video package and that I wanted someone to tell me how they could better spend $30 as a family. If they could, they would win the $30!

The great thing about it was every month some people would come and try to win the $30. I would ask if whatever they were suggesting was better than all the 65 channels that we provide. We would vote as a group and every time the group would vote down whatever somebody suggested.

What it did was reinforce in our employees mind that they were selling a very valuable package. The service was really important. So like I said hustle is believing in yourself and the business you're in.

The next hustle bullet point is:

KEEPING COMMITMENTS AND ENSURING TOTALLY SATISFIED CUSTOMERS.

That was a tough one.

Our mission statement - the third platform is, do what you say you're going to do.
If you tell somebody you are going to do something, you have to do it. If you didn't do it or you can't, it's up to you to go to your client and say here is why I can't do this or here is how I messed up. I apologize and won't let that happen again.

Having totally satisfied customers is one of the most difficult challenges a business can have. It's difficult with a few hundred or a thousand customers but it is particularly true in any industry where you potentially have hundreds of thousands of customers.

There is no question that it is an impossible task. However, any executive worth their salt should always shoot for perfection. Otherwise, what's the point? As Vince Lombardi said shoot for perfection and you'll end up with excellence.

We always shot for perfection and we measured our KPIs, our customer satisfaction in a variety of ways. Again the concept was that our customers were sitting at the table with us; that's the way we always looked at it.

Here is another Hustle bullet point:

HUSTLE IS ANSWERING CALLS IN THREE RINGS, AND BEING TOTALLY RESPONSIVE TO THE CALLER… EVEN WHEN IT'S NOT YOUR PHONE.

When I was a GM in Chicago, we had customer care sitting right outside my office; banks of phones and people. There were many times when I'd be walking through the office and a phone would be ringing but the CSR was in the bathroom, lunch or whatever. When that happened, I would stop and pick up the phone and say "Continental Cablevision how may help you…" Invariably, I would do whatever I had to and take care of whoever was on the other line.

By setting that example I was sending the message that every phone call is important. As an organization we can't just let the phone ring off the hook because it was somebody else's job to answer that phone. That is not the way to do it. You have to take the initiative, pick up the phone and ask, "How may I help you?"

Even if all you do is say, "I'm sorry they're not available at the moment but let me get your name and number and I will have them call you back directly." That goes a long way and often much farther than just getting voice mail sometimes.

The next Hustle bullet point:

HUSTLE IS PROVIDING TOP QUALITY SERVICE AND SUPPORT <u>ALL THE TIME</u>.

The best organizations don't just win some of the time or most of the time. Winning organizations must strive to win all of the time. If the organization is not focusing on providing excellent customer service all the time - back to the perfection thing – you are not getting the job done.

Remember Vince's words, "Perfection is not attainable, but if we chase perfection we can catch excellence".

If you shoot for perfection then you will end up with excellence; if you shoot for mediocrity you end up with crap.

I have seen many organizations that just say the enemy of best is good enough. That is a concept that I thoroughly reject. That's not the way to run any business.

Here is another Hustle bullet point:

HUSTLE IS HOPPING OUT OF BED LATE AT NIGHT TO WRITE DOWN A GREAT IDEA.

You always have to be prepared for a good idea and you never know when one is going to pop into your mind. Write it down AND THEN you can take the time to think it through. But write it down first the way it came to you; then think about it.

Dee could speak to this. She knows there were many times when I would go out for a run in the morning and then call her and say I had these ideas. Let's write them down…

> That's all very true. I remember the first time you came into Charter Communications. You walked in and started talking to me with all these ideas. I was just sitting there thinking what's he talking about?
>
> That is how I learned when you run, you get all these ideas and we both had to have paper and pencil ready at all times!
>
> ***Dee Speaks***

Here is another bullet point:

HUSTLE IS WHAT MAKES COMPANIES GREAT AND ELIMINATES THOSE WHO AREN'T.

Throughout the year I always emphasized that as we went into the third quarter, there is no score as unimportant as the score at halftime.

Okay we had a good first half but now we really have to get all over hustle. As we came out in the third quarter there were five things that I put in front of the team:

- First, come out fighting.

What I meant was let's not sit back on our laurels and think that we can cruise through the second half of the year and into the end zone. That's simply not going to happen. We have got to be hungrier than we were the first half of the year. We have to come out of the locker room fighting for every inch of everything we want.

The way we did that was by being very aggressive in our marketing campaigns. Again, think football; we would run plays we were running in the first half of the year and continue to execute our gameplan.

- Second, is execute, execute, execute and execute.

Here's where I got to tell my age old story which I know my people got tired of hearing. But they were polite and let me ramble on!

The story is about John McKay, who was the coach of the Tampa Bay Buccaneers. At the end of a game some interviewer asked what he thought of his team's execution. His reply was succinct, "I think it's a good idea!"

Execution is what separates winners from those in second, third and other places down the line. Everybody else talks a good game. Everybody else says they are going to do this stuff. But we do it - we execute it. When we do it, we do it right.

- Third was, hold 'em back, hold 'em back, hold 'em way back.

That was all about making sure our competition was not getting any interceptions on us. Staying on top of our competition was key and we always tried to understand what the competition was doing. Our research was ongoing. We were always looking up everything we could to see what packages and pricing they were doing. We always wanted to make sure they were not undercutting us. Our goal was to never let them get a foothold in any way, shape or form over what we were doing.

- Fourth is the quarterback sneak

We actually had a couple new plays in our gameplan that we put in that we called the quarterback sneak. As we got near the end of third quarter and we needed to make sure we hit our numbers, we put in that play.

Our quarterback sneak was a marketing campaign that we didn't have in the overall marketing plan. We had a month by month marketing plan but we left ourselves the ability to do other types of plays.

Everybody got a kick out of it because it was a football term and they could envision it. They could see the quarterback diving into the end zone to get the score.

- Fifth and the last was score often.

This was the pile-on theory. We used to talk a lot about piling on. Don't be happy with getting the score, getting ahead of budget by this amount. No - get ahead of budget 2X or 3X! Pile on, pile on, pile on! During the year unexpected problems arise and things happen. So even if you have a great lead something else can pop up and take that lead away from you quickly. So just keep piling on to make sure that at the end of the day nothing is going to come and take away our lead. We absolutely didn't ever want to relinquish our lead at any time! By this point our focus was the red-zone and the end zone at the end of the fourth quarter!

Take-Aways from Chapter 9

- HUSTLE!!
- Go for high touch customer service – always.
- Believe in your product.
- Do what you say you are going to do…always!

Interviews with Team Members and Partners

I learned so much from my Father. He was born in New York City of Italian parents, but since his mother didn't like it over here, they moved back to Italy when he was 6 months old. My dad came back when he was 13 years old and about a year later went to work with his uncles who were in the tile business.

My father became a tile-setter, eventually became the superintendent of a tile construction company. He was a self-made man and even handled the mosaic at the Kennedy Center. He would always treat everyone with respect, whether they were laborers or business owners. My dad and Coach Shula always used to tell me to make sure that I knew what was going on.

It was the best advice I ever received. When I was a sophomore in high school, he told me that he would be there for me. But he also said that he would help me decide on a course of action, but never tell me what to do. That way, he said, I couldn't blame somebody else and that I had to take responsibility for my actions.

Bob DeMarco
Past Center, St. Louis Cardinals, Dolphins, Browns, Rams

Interview with Team Members and Partners

> Working with Bill was interesting on many levels.
>
> What I would like to think is that I came out of my shell. It's not that that I've ever been a shy person, but working with Bill helped me to learn to push a little harder. I learned not be afraid to say, "I've hit a wall and need some help."
>
> I also learned how to bring others in even if the relationship wasn't as strong as I'd like it to be. I learned that you've not done your best if you stopped at the wall you've hit. Get some help and try to get around the wall! Then you've done the best you could.
>
> One other thing I learned was to be five minutes early for every call! It's become engrained in me! Bill taught us that we were late if we weren't five minutes early for every call!
>
> **Terie Hannay**
> **Past Regional Director, Customer Care, Charter Communications, Michigan**

Interview with Team Members and Partners

> Here is a clear example of what I mean. We had a great time working with Bill and his football theme. It was intense, but a great time and we got used to having fun, working hard and getting huge results.
>
> In the year after Bill was promoted and transferred, we had a new Regional Vice President take his place. It was as different as night and day.
>
> As soon as the new RVP came on board, he dismantled what Bill put in place. Everyone was demoralized because we knew there was a better way. We knew that everybody could work together, hit our goals and all pull toward the same goal line.
>
> It was the most opposite environment I could imagine. It was a fear environment instead of a positive team environment. "If there is a problem, blame it on the person over there…"
>
> To be perfectly honest, I should have walked out. We did it, but it is something I won't live through again.
>
> **Terie Hannay**
> **Past Regional Director, Customer Care, Charter Communications, Michigan**

CHAPTER TEN
THIRD QUARTER – CLIMBING THE MOUNTAIN

To me, the effort that needs to be expended in Q3 is almost like you're climbing a mountain.

The whole point is that as you are getting into Q3; you are now getting close enough to almost see the summit. The last thing you want to do is slip and slide your way back to the base of the mountain so you need to keep the pressure on. Work smart, work hard, work the gameplan and continually look for ways to beat your budget. And keep piling on, particularly in Q3 and Q4!

At this point in the game, if we're not already in a good position, then we have a really tough mountain to climb. Think of it in terms of a football game: you're coming out of halftime and you are down 31 to 0. That's really bad news. Teams can come back from that kind of deficit but digging yourself out of that hole is pretty tough. But what if you come out of halftime and your team owns the 31 score and your opponent has 0? Even then you can't take your foot off the accelerator. If you do, you open the door to disaster. Instead, I want to keep piling on and finish the game 85 to 0. We want to have a complete shut out and just smoke the scoreboard. That's the message we sent all the time.

Our hustle mantra was something we kept in mind all the time but particularly during the third and fourth quarters. It's important to stick to your mantra and gameplan but be flexible to take advantages of weakness in your competition or the market place. This was how we did it. It was our underlying philosophy - although we peppered in some Vince Lombardi and Bo Schembechler-isms here and there.

Some of the concepts we learned from Bo Schembechler during our halftime in Michigan was spot-on. At different times, I would put out e-mails reminding the team about some critical things to remember.

Most of my job was to make sure the gameplan was being followed. I did much of that through our daily calls during which I would continually make sure that our customer service was top-notch.

Another part of our plan was to make sure the team was not just properly motivated but properly incentivized, too.

Every organization has tough times. When that happened to us, I would send along personal notes or e-mails from time to time just to let everybody know that I knew what was going on. I wanted to make sure that they knew that I was a part of it and understood what was happening. In the end, I believe that was a big part of our success.

People want to know that their leader in the organization is plugged in. I mean really plugged in not just superficially plugged in.

Early in my career there was a guy whose nickname around the company was "Mr. Excellent." People called him "Mr. Excellent" because every time he would see somebody he would say, "You're excellent!" He thought he was motivating people and telling them they were excellent no matter what was going on. The problem was that he had no clue what they were doing or how they were performing. Regardless, he would always tell them they were "excellent."

That lesson taught me that I needed to be very careful how I would pick my opportunities to send an e-mail or call somebody to let them know that they were doing a really good job. We didn't "blow smoke..." but instead our approach was to get our point across.

I was always careful to watch and observe the energy level of the team as well as individual team members. When a team member or the entire team seemed to be stressed out, I'd shift gears and lighten things up. All work and no play... as the saying goes!

Once a month we would have our all-employee meetings. At those meetings we would have giveaways, such as box tickets to baseball games, hockey games and other similar events. We would also highlight the employee of the month. If someone did something above and beyond we would call them up and give them an award in front of everybody. It's important to recognize a team member's big-time efforts. Without these types of efforts, creativity and energy, closing the gap on our goals would be just that much more difficult.

But without a doubt, we also had fun, lots of fun and we did fun stuff all the time. When I ran the Central Region in St Louis, I put an actual football field down in our regional office in St. Louis. The field was about 30 feet wide by about 100 feet long. We had to have a goal post at both ends... of course! Stripes too – how can you have a football field without a 50 yard line! During the day, we'd often go out there and kick field goals. Sometimes we'd have contests to see who could kick the farthest field goal or run the best pass patterns! Building maintenance was getting frustrated with us because several times we kicked the ceiling lights out...oops!

When my regional managers would come to our offices we'd sometimes break up into smaller teams, go to the parking lot and play football or shoot baskets. I know it's hard to believe but this was normal for us. We did all kinds of fun things to keep things loose.

Don't get me wrong, we were very serious about hitting our budget and goals. In fact, I introduced what I called "stretch goals" from day one. I called the stretch goal the goal. I have always been a big believer in aiming high and hitting high.

But in every organization, there's always a smart-aleck or two. I had a guy in one of my organizations who twisted my words and use to tell his team like Bill says aim low, miss low... No, I meant aim high, hit high!

So I always made it clear **that the stretch goal is the goal**. That's where we are going. If you chase perfection you'll end up with excellence. I always knew if we chased the stretch goals, the worst that would happen is that we would hit our budgeted goals. The gameplan was simple, we would hit our budgeted goals and we win. But we always chased our stretch goals from day one and many were surprised just how many times we exceeded our budgeted goals by a bunch!

The reason this worked is because I didn't just talk about our goals from a company point of view. I always talked about what it meant to the team and each team member personally. This was a constant theme throughout the year and I kept reiterating that concept until it became part of the fabric of the company.

I found myself frequently going back to Vince Lombardi's quote:

> *"The quality of a person's life is directly proportional to their commitment to excellence regardless of their field of endeavor."*

Our focus was always that what we had was an opportunity to do great things for our families.

I obviously didn't know what each individual needed or wanted for themselves and their families. All of us go through trials and tribulations, but here and now was an opportunity to earn additional money and help provide a better life for our families. Of course, the extra funds could make you a hero in the eyes of your family. But it would also help you with money for a new house, for the kids going to college or whatever. I would always talk about our success and achievements in terms of what it meant to their families - and much less frequently about what it meant to the company.
Let's be honest, a lot of people care about the company, they want the company to be successful but I have always considered that to be a basic premise. What really motivates people and gets high performance is when they understand what it means to their team, to them and to their families.

Throughout all of this there was a strong message. It was "the team." I always spoke in terms of our organization as a team. Team members don't leave other team members dangle in the wind; we don't let each other down and just as in the military, there is no person left behind.

If there's somebody in the organization that is failing or is having a hard time, we as a team pick that person up or pick up that position and carry it along into the end zone. This is a core lesson in the U.S. military. It's a Navy Seal thought process.

We would "peel the onion" back – starting with the team and work our way back to the individual members. It makes it personal for each team member when each person understands the importance of each individual member's efforts. In the end, each person would eventually recognize that the team couldn't exist without the individual members. They also realized that each member was much stronger, more effective and much more efficient when they belonged to a team.

Eventually, that thinking permeated through the hearts and minds of each team member. In the end, they didn't want to let their teammates down and they didn't want to miss their goals. They were part of the Charter Michigan Blizzard or they were part of the Charter Central Cyclone. They were part of the team and knew they wanted to win.

And they knew they wanted to win the Super Bowl.

But all that didn't occur overnight. In fact, a lot of it was honestly due to the efforts of the senior team. My senior team included Dee and my direct reports. I told them from the beginning that it was not going to be simple or easy putting this entire organization and team together. Nor was it going to be something that was a fly-by-night organization. I made sure that everyone understood that this was something we had to
live - all the time.

To build the team we had to constantly talk about team skills, team opportunities, team goals and constantly be talking team. When the rubber hit the road I couldn't have some of my regional leaders heading down some private or personal road. Nor would I permit them to get in front of their team and yell at them because "you are making me look bad!" That might be someone else's concept of a team but it certainly was not mine! Instead, it would take a constant effort to make sure that everybody knew we had to stick to the team concept. We had to talk about team, team and team!

To keep our momentum high, we continually did things and had events that would perpetuate the "team" thinking. When we had our personal meetings, the team members had to wear their jerseys, with their names on them, of course! In the beginning, each team member had a position and there was a lot of communication.

I would often go to their monthly meetings and send e-mails to the entire management team. I did that whether they were across the state of Michigan, throughout the Central region or throughout the division when I ran it.

When one quarter was getting close to ending, I would send out an email that would set the stage for this transition. I always stayed in character - always. I never got out of character. I was always Coach Shreffler and everybody looked at me that way. My teammates and regional leaders called me Coach because I stayed in character. All that helped because I wanted to set the stage and let people know I was serious, that this was the team and this was what we were going to do.

I didn't go in and out of character when it suited me. I figured I had to stay in it and see it through. Staying in character was a very big commitment.

There were many times when it wasn't easy. Although sometimes in business you just want to lose it, but "public beatings are never good." You do those in private. Never, ever scold people in public. Reserve that for private sessions and always do it in non-emotional terms. The correct approach is here's the gameplan and here's where we're going. I did a lot of that. You don't want your teammate remembering how much they despise you because you yelled at them. You want them to remember what resulted from their actions and how it hurt the team. Look inward, not outward.

Silence, used properly, is extremely effective. Learn how to use silence the right way.

I remember my dad telling me a story when I was a kid. My father was a manger of accounting for US Steel for many years. One of the guys that reported to my dad often told his fellow workers that when my dad was loud, he was in a good mood. But when my dad was upset, my dad would get really quiet and spoke very softly. When that happened, they knew he was upset.

I learned to use that technique when we had our daily call. If I had some team members that were not executing or carrying his or her weight, this simple phrase worked unbelievably well. It sent the message to everybody on the call that, "oh-oh, Bill is ticked." All I would say - leaning into the phone - was "give me a call right after this call." It was loud and clear and better than yelling and screaming. Everybody knew right away, "oh-oh", they are going to have a talk about what is going on.

It occurred to me that when you were putting everything together you were very consistent and clear in relating your gameplan and expectations to everyone. In addition, your behavior, whether in private, public, celebrations, serious meetings was consistent so that everyone in the company came to know what to do and consequentially was not surprised when one of them was called to task.

Like you said, you never let it slip. That is really critical and hard to do but it also worked because people react to that sort of thing. They come around and react well because no player likes to disappoint the coach.

Most players want to see their coach as enthusiastic. If he isn't enthusiastic, he is not happy and something is wrong. When something is wrong you can bet your bottom dollar that it will be directed at you.

All of that stuff you did and everything you continued to do becomes more and more effective. Just like your changing tone of voice – it all becomes part of your coaching role.

If you were just a manager in a regular organization and being the coach was not part of your character, then it would be far less effective. It would mean much less to most people. And if you started screaming and yelling then people would begin to think, "What the hell does he want?"

But when you tell them to call you after the phone meeting, like you said, they know something is very wrong.

JACKIE'S PERSPECTIVE

You are exactly right Jackie.

You need to send a message loud and clear to the rest of your managers. As a coach or leader you do not have to get into a screaming and yelling match. You just simply say we're going to have this talk in private because nobody wants to be beaten up in public either.

> Well no, but you had built enough respect for them. Again you set the stage with your consistency.
>
> ## JACKIE'S PERSPECTIVE

It's now late in the third quarter and as the clock winds down, I'm beginning to send email messages to prepare for the celebration. The message also says that we still have to pile on, hustle and pile on some more. But by hitting our goals – our stretch goals - we should begin to prepare to have fun. When we do, we'll look back with pride and we'll celebrate the fantastic year we are having.

So get ready - it's coming.

We have one more quarter - pile on! Keep all the mojo going - we are getting close. I can smell it - you can smell it - we are almost there - don't give up.

That was the message. I always tried to paint the positive picture.

I used to tell the team, you will never hear me say "I hate to lose" because they are two negatives. Hate is a bad word and lose is a worse word.

Instead, I would say "I love to win" - because those are two positive words.

In this organization we don't talk about hating or lose; we talk about loving and win.
I would say we are getting close. We love to win. We will have a big party. We are going have a blast.

You will tell your family about this for decades to come and about the team you are on.
Just keep it going - keep it going. Push hard - hit your goals. Run the quarterback sneak!   Run all the plays. And if there's something else you got that we don't have, get out and go get it. The test is now – it all comes down to doing it now!

And as the buzzer goes off, the long pass is in the air. Our wide receiver is running flat out, chased closely by our competition. But our wide receiver looks over his right shoulder and lets the perfectly thrown pass drop into his open arms… and now it's the end of the third quarter!

Key Take-Aways from Chapter 10

- Remain flexible and look for every opportunity to win.
- Be sincere in your praise – don't be Mr. Excellent!
- Have fun.
- Repeat third bullet point over and over.
- Aim high – hit high!
- Remember to think about your teammate's families.
- Don't be afraid to pile on!!

Interviews with Team Members and Partners

> People who study organization behavior will tell you that there is a fairness quotient that people are always balancing. Employees are always asking themselves whether or not they are giving more to the company than they are getting.
>
> You want to be in the "sweet spot." That's the point where people aren't so concerned. They know if the company does well, the company and their bosses are going to take care of them. Here's the process:
>
> - They know how much money they are making.
> - They know what's expected of them, (KPIs).
> - They know or should know the bonus structure.
>
> After that, they don't have to think about that anymore. If they and their co-workers hit their goals, then they will all look like heroes.
>
> In those other organizations, employees start to bring the fairness question to the front burner. When they do, turnover goes up and so does employee jealousy. "I'm doing this and this other guy is not doing that..."
>
> Regardless of culture or upbringing, fairness and equity are really just innate human traits. If people feel they are being treated unfairly, they take steps to shift the balance.
>
> In other words they leave the company, withhold performance, and do things that will have adverse consequences on what the company is trying to accomplish.
>
> Bill's organizations had none of those negatives and all of the positives.
>
> **Mike Wylie, past Suddenlink CAO, CFO Broadstripe and current CFO Pulse Broadband**

Interviews with Team Members and Partners

> I think you have a goal and you keep working toward that goal. In football I never once thought practice was hard, I loved doing it, I really enjoyed the competition you had every day and that was fun. So to me, in business people generally complain about some of the hard work and hours and I have to laugh and respond they just don't know what hard work is. There is nothing much harder than pro football.
>
> **Taz Anderson**
> **Past All American Fullback at Georgia Tech, Tight end St. Louis Cardinals and the Atlanta Falcons**

> It wasn't all peaches and cream. There definitely were some struggles; we all worked very hard and we understood what was expected.
>
> I would say that on average, we worked eight to nine hours at the office, and another hour or two after that for number crunching and the planning. It wasn't 14 hours a day, it was about 10 hours. It was very intense, and it was an exceptionally productive 10 hours.
>
> **Terie Hannay**
> **Past Regional Director, Customer Care, Charter Communications, Michigan**

CHAPTER ELEVEN
FOURTH QUARTER –

EXECUTING, RED ZONE, THIRD-DOWN CONVERSIONS, KPIS AND BRINGING IT ALL "HOME"

> In general, the "prevent" defense is designed to keep the offense from making a big play that can win the game. It can be used in any obvious passing situation but especially when the offense must score to win.
>
> It's called the "prevent" defense because the defense wants to "prevent" a receiver from getting behind them and catching a pass for a score in such obvious passing situations. When utilizing this defense, teams may substitute players from "skilled" positions; players more agile, faster and more capable of defending against these obvious passing situations.
>
> **JACKIE'S PERSPECTIVE**

When you are ahead and the score is in your favor, don't forget what it took to get you there; don't start resting on your success. Stay on offense, keep moving and stay alert. Especially when you're behind, stay on offense while time is on your side. Either way stay positive because it sends the right message to players on the team AND the players on defense. **No matter what, stay in the game until the buzzer.**

All too often when a team is ahead by a meaningful margin, there is a tendency to sit back, shift into neutral and wait for the end of the game, quarter or year. Sometimes the team moves to a "prevent defense" when the situation does not call for it. If that happens, the chances are the team will lose the game.

The opponents will quickly spot the weakness. In football, the offense will then quickly go back to the running game, since the prevent defense has a minimum of rushers, so the running backs can eat up lots of yardage. You are probably not going to win games with such tactics.

It all comes back to the gameplan....and common sense.

Everything that we've talked about earlier in this book is that we were laying the groundwork for key performance indicators for specific goals. KPIs are specific and measurable goals; the foundation of your team and gameplan. That's because we are trying to be very specific so we can achieve very specific results.

Third-down conversions are essential to winning games, and they are equally essential to winning at business.
In a very real sense three-and-out is a losing strategy. Three-and-out means you lose the ball and now you have to play defense. Don't get me wrong, a good defense is crucial to the game's outcome. But it's hard to rack up points and win a game if all you are doing is playing defense! That said, defense gives you the ability to get back into the game.

From a business perspective, if your plan was to grow by 50 customers this week and you only gained 20, that deficit takes away your options. Next week, just to get your plan to break even you need to find 80 new customers.

That's a 60% increase over this week's performance. Now you have to do some type of special marketing campaign to make up the difference. That special marketing campaign probably will cost you some extra money, which eats into the profits. It also will take more technicians, too. Then, to get back to the same profit levels you need even more sales. It's all a vicious circle when the team "under-executes."

Just like in football, "three and out" says you are losing ground, are not able to follow the gameplan and losing your options. Third and long is the same situation; you lose your flexibility and options.

As this causes the business unit to have to do more things, spend more money and increase sales even more to make up for the added costs. **If it is going to be more expensive to get to your goal why not just execute better in the first place.** Track and hit your KPIs. Make sure your goals are happening so you don't have to face that third and long play or third-down conversion. The odds for successful execution fall when that happens.

All of this helped me to talk about why we don't want to go three-and-out. That's my way of saying hit your numbers, move the ball, keep things going, move down the field, get in the red zone and we are going to score.

> Successful third down conversions obviously keep the opponents offensive team off the field.
>
> Third down plays, like other plays, are designed after studying opponents in similar down-and-distance situations, trying to anticipate what the defense will come up with. Teams spend a lot of time trying to anticipate what the defense will run while the defense is trying to anticipate the offenses anticipation! (I'm so confused!) Just as in business, these "third down situations" are critical to keep the team moving down the field; consequently, teams spent a lot of practice time on their execution.
>
> Winning teams have a history of third down conversions. Their goal is to simply take as much time as possible with a well conceived game play and score a touchdown….and then, do it again… and again…
>
> The best offense, the winning team, converts third down situations.
>
> **JACKIE'S PERSPECTIVE**

The issue really is keeping your offense on the field. Third down conversions are just part of that strategy and mindset. Jackie is right, of course. By not going three-and-out, you keep your team on the field and moving the ball down the field.

The opposite happens with your opponent. They are forced to continue to play defense and their backs keep getting closer and closer to your goal line. In the Red Zone, your opponents eventually run out of maneuvering room. That dramatically increases their chances for failure – and your chance for success.

Fourth quarter is also a crucial time to keep all your best players on the field. In football, injuries can take their toll and sideline your best players. That's why it's important to have a deep bench, in both sports and business. Everyone, even those on the bench must be ready at a moment's notice to take the field. Everyone must know and understand the gameplan. Everyone must know and understand their goals and objectives. Everyone must know and understand what specifically is being asked of them.

The gameplan, the marketing plan and the marketing campaign – almost always needs to be tweaked a little.

For example what if you are running into a major competitor that suddenly got a new product or technological edge that you don't have? Obviously, you have to make some adjustments. Huddle with your team and get their input. We did this every day during our daily call. Those calls were for talking about not just the numbers but all the other things that crop up and could become hurdles. Solving and responding to problems or unforeseen situations is much easier when they are new or small instead of entrenched and large!

Huddles are also for talking about execution, making it happen and what is important. My experience is that huddling is what really moves the ball; it's what gets everybody focused and heading in the same direction. The daily call was our huddle.

The message is simple: staying on top of the situation and not fumbling or dropping the ball keeps the offense on the field. Intensity is important and it is a crucial part of the process. Whether it is football or business, you have to have a strong commitment to your team and to your business unit.

To do that, you have to believe in yourself, your team and that you and your team are going to be successful. It's no secret - everything always gets back to having the right attitude.

Attitude is everything.

We used to tell everybody attitudes are important – 'is yours worth catching?' If you start off with a great attitude and build from there, you make sure your teammates have that same attitude, too. If you come in to work dragging your feet, you won't have that intensity. When that happens and you can't overcome that feeling, then it's time to find another job. Love it or leave it is really the only path to success. All those hurdles are tough enough to overcome, even when you have a good attitude!

Those that believe in their hearts and souls that this is the right mission are the ones who will achieve the most. Hurdles, while high, often don't seem as insurmountable when the team stays focused on the goal.

It's all about having that intensity and belief.

Everybody on the team must be living and breathing the gameplan. That way, everyone is continually pushing in the same direction. If you don't, you have a varied interest among the team and you will not be successful. Sure, you may have some wins, you might convert a couple third downs and you might be on the field for now but you're not going to consistently score. Instead, it's the high-performing team that is going to score much more often when they get their hands on the ball.

In the business world like on the field, we constantly have to watch the competition. They are watching us so we need to watch them. Our team members would watch what our competition was doing and then report back about what they observed. All of that was part of our daily huddle. We would always talk about the things our competition was doing as well as what our customers are saying. We also paid attention to what our customers were asking for, were frustrated with or just commenting on.

It's often just the little things that are very important. Listening and learning was part of our critical focus. When we did that well, we generally scored every time. When we didn't, we opened the door to fumbling and letting our competition grab the ball and run.

> In the short year I was with the Cowboys, I was simply amazed at the plays Coach Landry conceived. I never had another coach with such ability to produce unique plays...and plays that worked... if the players did their part. And like all good leaders, we had that confidence in him. If we executed the plays he called, chances are we would win.
>
> Each week would start by watching the game played the previous Sunday.
> Watching the game film, not videos like it is nowadays, of Sunday's game was for observing how individuals performed and how fundamentals could be improved.
>
> So the game film was useful for making corrections for future games. In preparation for the next game, we also filmed individual segments like the linemen, the receivers, or linebackers. With this type of detailed filming we were able to make small, but critical, adjustments in blocking, receiving or positioning. Success in football, like in business, is really in the details. Everyone can play, but when it's a game of inches or timing, attention to details dictate the winner.
>
> Each team has coaches in the press box on game day. Their job is to determine if the teams are reacting as anticipated and, if not, make some suggestions. The ability to observe and make effective changes in the gameplan is critical. The other team is anticipating what you may be doing and will be trying to offset it. Coaches have to be aware that's happening and react accordingly. Many game winning plays have been drawn up in the press box or on the sidelines. Being strong and fast is critical, but many games are won from the neck up.
>
> **JACKIE'S PERSPECTIVE**

If you want to win you have to look inward. If you don't look inward and just say, okay I am the manager, I'm the boss and tomorrow we are going to start winning. Look out. It won't work.

All too often, bosses leave in their own existing management philosophy and attitudes. Some go so far as to say "there is the highway and anyone who doesn't perform is out". When that happens, the boss is often the one that losses and is not going anywhere. That's the definition of insanity: doing the same thing over and over and expecting different results.

Again, it's all about the foundation that a manager, a boss, a CEO or any leader builds.
Ninety eight percent of those who are reading this book or other books like it will be better prepared to go through a management-style sea-change. That's the kind of change you will need to take your operation to an entirely new level of productivity and commitment. .

The way we think about things is crucial to our levels of success. What's really great is that all this can be learned and put into action with a bit of continuing effort.

I used to love to ask my managers, "Who likes to tell somebody they are not doing a good job?" No one ever raised their hand. Indeed, everybody hates to tell somebody they're not doing a good job.

Then I would change the question and ask, "Who likes to tell your teammate they are doing a great job?" Every hand went up. Then I would ask, "How many have told any single teammate in the last 30 days that they were doing a great job?" All hands, with the exception of one or maybe two went down.

Once again it is all about training people on how to have a winning organization. Not – "the beatings will continue until morale improves!"

The fourth quarter, the Red Zone and third-down conversions are all about executing to high degrees. It's about piling on and hitting all the KPIs. It's about winning and having fun.

If I can do it, so can you. Like me, you just have to find a way that works really well for you. I found mine in my thematic, goal oriented business plan. I connected my working-adult with my inner-child and developed a process that clearly worked… and changed many of our lives along the way.

In the next chapters, we'll pass along a few more ideas. Stay tuned!

Key Take-Aways from Chapter 11

- Don't go "three-and-out".
- Keep your best players on the field – everyone needs to know and understand the gameplan.
- Believe, really believe, you will be successful.
- Allow yourself a 'sea change' in your thinking.

Interviews with Team Members

> From a corporate standpoint, you want to take best practices and share those with friends and colleagues. I found it really interesting that only one other regional VP at Charter embraced Bill's underlying philosophy and execution given his success with the program in Michigan. Everyone has their own style and way of doing business, but I was amazed more didn't use its underlying fundamentals to help lead change and results.
>
> I think it helped me to see that there is nothing to lose by embracing it and trying it. I was fortunate to learn early on the value it can bring to an organization that you manage.
>
> **Jim Holanda, CEO – RCN/Choice Cable**

> One other important thing I learned from Bill was that if I were running an organization, the only way to succeed is in a team environment. It doesn't whether it is a football theme or some other type of theme, - if you don't take down the walls, you can't reach the highest success.
>
> You can't survive as a company without measurements, so the KPIs have to be a number one priority. Regardless of what type of company it is, there is always something that is measurable.
>
> You have to define your goals. What is the expectation? Where are you at today?
>
> You have to get that in place first, and then really keep pushing in whatever way you can. You have to break down the walls and get the entire organization moving towards the goal.
>
> All too often, people really don't believe that a budget is a budget, and that the budget goals can be met or exceeded. As a leader, Bill is one of the best. He's an eternal optimist and always there to support you no matter what.
>
> **Terie Hannay**
> **Past Regional Director, Customer Care, Charter Communications, Michigan**

Interviews with Team Members

> A program like Bill's KPI system provides a rich internal reporting structure. It takes a lot of work, but once you get the data reporting systems up and running, the number of reports and availability of data make internal and external reporting very easy.
>
> Senior management and private investors generally want to see some different things. With the right system, all the data they want is really a summary or subset of the internal data. Since Bill's KPIs focus on 8 or 10 key areas for each department, the data collection system creates most all of the data that is required.
>
> It also makes compliance in public companies much easier. I didn't have to spend a tremendous amount of time and resources on an external reporting, because I just basically had to summarize a subset of my internal reports. These reports were so complete and integrated that it streamlined the process.
>
> That gets you into part of limiting surprises. Managing with the KPIs became significantly easier – both internally and externally. It minimized surprises with a clear set of expectations and goals.
>
> **Mike Wylie, past Suddenlink CAO, CFO Broadstripe and current CFO Pulse Broadband**

CHAPTER TWELVE
THE FINAL DRIVE BEGINS

It's almost the end of the 4th quarter, the end of the game and it is the end of the year.

Without exaggeration, it was the culmination of a year where Vince Lombardi's hallowed words echoed throughout our minds…

> *I firmly believe that any man's finest hour, the greatest fulfillment of all that he holds dear, is that moment when he has worked his heart out in a good cause and lies exhausted on the field of battle – victorious.*

Very few have ever said it better than that.

When all this began, my team and I developed a three year plan. In the first year, our goal was to win the Division – or in our case hit our budgeted goals. The second year goal was to win the Conference – which we defined as beating each of our budgeted goals. Our third year was to win the Super Bowl – which meant that we wanted to be the top division in the company and beat each of our budgeted goals by 5%.

During the last month and the last weeks the management team became tremendous cheerleaders.

We cheered on the parts of the organization that were hitting on all cylinders: go, go, go! We also knew which parts of the organization were not doing quite as well and were lagging behind. So we needed the parts of the organization that were executing and exceeding their goals to keep pushing and bring home the bacon. That way, the efforts of the real performers would offset the ones that weren't doing so well – or doing the best that they could at the time.

We were handing the ball off to our proven players – our best running backs and wide receivers. We knew we could rely on them to execute their plan and drive the ball across the goal line. Redzone-failure was not in their vocabulary!

During that last month, every Daily Call and meeting was all about where we needed to be at the end of the year. We are almost there; we are in the red zone, we are ready to score. We knew we were going to win the year but we wanted everyone to keep going - keep going – keep going. Each Daily Call and meeting became a rah-rah session in the last month of each of those years.

During those calls and meetings, I would often tell motivational stories about some of the famous drives in NFL history. John Elway of the Broncos was well known for last minute drives. It was the same thing with Joe Montana. These guys were quarterbacks in the true sense of the word. With minutes left in the game, it was a well-known fact that if you gave Elway or Montana the ball, they would take it down the field, giving their team the opportunity to win.

It's the same thing in business. You make sure you put the ball in the hands of your teammates that you feel are going to score. They know what they need to do to get the job done. So we gave them the ball and let them go for that big drive. When we did, they would get in there and score. They were our "go-to" people!

One of our operations along the lake in Grand Haven, Michigan is a perfect example. Our GM, Dan Spoelman and his group were doing very well. They were hitting their KPIs and exceeding their customer growth targets. Their financial success was strong, too, so Dan and his group became our first Most Valuable Players (MVPs).

Throughout the year, we identified certain people and organizations that were at the top of their games. These were our MVPs. Dan and his team were moving the ball and moving the chains (meaning getting first downs) every day. They were a great example of winners! In particular, they were great examples of what we were trying to achieve.

When the subject of our MVPs comes up, the conversation often turns to what the MVPs were doing differently than the other groups.

In Dan's case, he completely embraced what we were trying to achieve. But more importantly, he tried to make it his own. He took our football concept and built his team around it. Dan's focus was laser-like, as was his follow up, but the key was his great attitude. He embraced the totality of our system and had a blast doing it.

Another important point was that we always strived to teach and manage in a positive, not negative way. For example, we taught the concept that "I will win and never give up." We never said "we hate to lose" because that had a negative tone to it.

Once you introduce negative elements into your leadership style, things can go downhill quickly. All too often, managers sense that it is easier to manage using negative motivations and scare tactics. We never did that. Instead, we always said – and taught - the positive. We would always say, "I love to win", never, "I hate to lose."

Dan embraced it, grabbed it and ran! But he didn't stop there. Dan took the concept of the football team and drove it all the way down and through his organization. He had folks in his organization that had sub-teams and tee shirts that had their sub-team names printed on them. He completely embraced everything we were teaching and trying to achieve. What was special about Dan was that in his own way, he made it come to life and it was a pleasure to watch it happen.

From our position, the difference Dan was making was clear. Let's say you had five regions and Dan's region was leading the pack. The lessor performing divisions below Dan's were not embracing the Michigan Blizzard concept and theme in the same way or to the same extent. Yes, when they were on our Daily Call, they somewhat embraced the concept and were doing what we asked them to do. In the end, Dan's group had that *"special something."*

We eventually realized that the difference was the lessor performing regions weren't making the concept their own. Dan and his group were not just doing what we asked them to do; they were also going above and beyond what we were asking them to do.

On the other hand, when we identified people that regularly went above and beyond, the first thing we did was to congratulate them on the Daily Call and highlight their efforts. Next, we would make them the MVPs for the entire region.

Then the fun started. Once we identified and acknowledged their efforts, we would bring them to the regional office and attend our staff meetings. At these meetings, we would ask them their direct feedback on how we could improve as an organization.

All this really got them into the guts of what we were trying to achieve. By actively and honestly seeking their feedback, they became a part of improving our overall operations. These MVPs were our winners. They were people who knew how to get their jobs done well and in a positive way. They had the best ideas so our job was to learn from them.

While they were at the regional office - and everybody knew they were coming - we would take them out to lunch with the regional team to talk to them and thank them. They would receive their own MVP plaque and their entire time at the regional office would be an event.

I would also go to their all employee meetings and deliver the plaque in front of their co-workers. This helped their coworkers realize we were identifying one of their own.

Again, it is back to recognition. We wanted to recognize our MVPs in a particular way. When you point to the people that do well, they get elevated to a whole different level. The rest of the organization then sees what is going on and many decide they want to be in that MVP category, too. They want to be that person.

Each operation would have their own group MVP's and identify these MVP's at their all- employee meeting. These MVP recipients would extend further down into each organization into positions like the front line technicians or the installers. Each operation leader would hand out a shirt or a plaque for a particular month and thank them for their efforts. Our MVP program reached multi-levels throughout the organization.

We also found that our underperforming operational groups were consistently **NOT doing** what the successful groups **WERE doing**. Recognition was lacking and management by fear or neglect was pervasive. In sort, the managers of those groups were not embracing our overall concept. In particular, they didn't embrace the football theme or our positive management approach. Some thought our football concept was silly and beneath their dignity. Others thought that keeping their management style positive was a waste of time.

In one situation, I found where a GM didn't hand out the jerseys. He came to a regional meeting and told everyone they named the team and they were having a great time. But within a few months it was clear that his group was severely lagging behind the top performing groups.

During one of our on-site visits, we discovered that his team didn't know what we were talking about when we brought up our football concept and theme. As a result, they were missing a lot of the fun as well as their numbers - big time. We also discovered that they had made up their budget on a whim. It was a disaster and it occurred at Broadstripe.

In Michigan I had a group that didn't embrace the concept either. Morale was poor throughout that organization and didn't get any better despite our initial efforts. They had the mindset, "you can't tell me anything. We've been running operations for a long time, so don't tell me what to do..." From their perspective, they were giving it their best.

The problem was that their "best" was sub-par and trailed all the other groups. More importantly, all the rest of the region had to make up for them. We were close enough to the end of the year that we decided that firing them right then wouldn't make any significant difference.

Charter had acquired this group through acquisitions in February/March of that year. It was one of the five acquisitions that created the Michigan Region.
Three months into the acquisition, it was clear that this group was not hitting their numbers. My team and I set up different mentoring systems with the leaders. However, the problem was that what they were telling us and what they were doing were two different things.

By the time we had an opportunity to really dig in the problems, we discovered they were not embracing our strategy, nor were they telling us the truth. But these guys really covered their tracks for a number of months – that was, until the truth was finally visible.

It all came to a head when we were preparing our budget for the next year. This team came to the budget review meeting, but didn't have their budget done. In fact, they came in without any thought or feedback and **told us to tell them what we wanted - and they would write it down**!

This was around November and we made the decision it was better to let their group limp into the end zone than to blow it all up right then. However, they were not going to be a part of the ongoing team. Despite all that, by the end of the year we still blew away our numbers for the region as a whole.

If anybody ever loses their job in an organization and it is a surprise, shame on senior management.

If you are a good senior manager and you are communicating what you expect, then everybody knows what is expected. If somebody gets fired and they act shocked about it, then shame on you as the leader. If that happens, you did not do a good job of communicating to them that they were not hitting your standards.

However, on January 2nd we did make the necessary changes. I made a quick visit with some of my key regional team members and we allowed the three top leaders to pursue "trainee" opportunities in the food services industry. In other words, we cut the head off the snake.

When those three people were ushered out of the building, each one had no doubt that this was coming and it was just a matter of time.

Immediately, the rest of the team jumped on board. Attitudes and morale changed quickly and we were happy to see all the changes. They didn't know about all the successes that were happening in the rest of the region. However, they knew what **was not** happening in their own operation.

Even a mediocre quarterback can complete some good passes and handoffs now and then. That's what happened in that situation. Eventually, you get wise to it. NO news is NOT good news. It's critical to always look behind the curtain. By our second year, we began to learn how to more quickly identify those who were not buying into our program. If you are not hearing anything, don't assume that everything is working!

In our case, we had our Daily Call, which let us closely track results – KPIs. But sometimes someone gets so good at BSing upper management that it's hard to detect reality from fiction. Regardless, eventually the numbers make everything clear.

By my third cycle, (Michigan, St. Louis, and finally Broadstripe), we had nailed the identification process. At Broadstripe, we had an operational leader that tried to scam us. But because of our prior experiences, our antenna was up and we shut down that effort much earlier.

Isn't it amazing how some people spend so much effort trying to get out of doing what they need to do?

I did the football theme three different times. Each time it worked like a champ because all the components came together, including the all-important half time and year end celebrations. All too often, leaders forget to celebrate their successes and keep everyone's nose to the grindstone.

Each of these three teams was with a different organization. The first was in Michigan in 2000. During that first year of my thematic approach, we, the Michigan Blizzard, blew our numbers away. In fact, we did such an outstanding job that we were on the cover of the 2000 Charter Communications Annual Report.

Unfortunately, after I left in March of 2001, the next management team eliminated my whole thematic concept. They didn't believe it was necessary. As a result they missed their budget and did not have a good year.

However, one group hit their numbers and practically carried the entire region. That was the group that did exceedingly well in the first year. What happened was that they learned the proper habits on how to run the business even though they were not allowed to continue the Michigan Blizzard theme. The team building skills they learned in that first year helped them to continue to keep their organization strong – despite the fact that they were bucking a pretty strong headwind and not able to use the Michigan Blizzard theme.

> As Bill just mentioned, once a group learns and implements key control and productivity techniques - creating a high performance organization becomes much easier. Two of those key elements are Bill's KPIs and the Daily Call. Together, these two go a long way towards dramatically enhancing the operational capacity of a business.
>
> That said, Bill's thematic approach adds the key missing ingredient to the standard, numbers-driven organization. This missing ingredient is the "honest to goodness fun" people can have while working.
>
> Unfortunately, "fun" is often the key element that is usually lacking in today's ultra-high productivity environment. Try it Bill's way and see what happens!
>
> ## Phil's Thoughts

In March 2001 I was promoted and went to the Central Region, which was an entirely different group of people. Once again, I initiated our football theme. In the end it again worked well, but the start was rocky.

When I was first brought down to St. Louis, Jerry Kent, the CEO and one of the founders of Charter Communication told me he wanted me to replicate what I did in Michigan. Charter was getting ready to acquire some AT&T properties and the region was going to get much bigger, very quickly. In effect, he said, "This is the mother ship and we really need you to do a great job."

Consequently, I started a bit behind the eight-ball. Many obviously knew about the Michigan Blizzard's success, but from day one I had to earn their respect.
The point is that I realized I could successfully apply this thematic process whether it was with a newly formed organization or a core part of an existing organization. I also found out that our thematic process could be implemented in about 30 days.

The recipe is:

- To hold the kickoff meeting where you rolled out the team.
- Next, you need to bring everybody in the room and talk about the business goals.
- Third, is to not let anyone leave until they come up with how they are going to beat those numbers by 5%.

We took notes and then held everyone to their goals, objectives and to those dollars. After that, you sent them out on an upbeat note with their team names and intense focus. It's critical to keep that fun atmosphere and intense focus from then on.

The Daily Call is what keeps the focus and fun intact. Every day, each person on the call would tell everyone what they did yesterday, what they are going to do today and what there are going to do tomorrow.

That is the recipe: The secret sauce; the winning formula. It's simple but effective.

This is what got us into that great position for the final drive.

In each case - Michigan, St. Louis and Broadstripe - I believe it was our thematic approach that helped to keep the fun alive. It also helped to translate what all too often becomes a "daily slog" into something that can be fun and motivational.

Indeed, this is how we did it. There is peer pressure but there are no public beatings. It is the carrot, it is not the stick. Everybody wants to be the producer and get a pat on the back, whether it was in person or on our Daily Call. More importantly, everybody tries harder to be in that position.

> That's true. Bill would sometimes ask who wanted to go first and it was always the group that was doing well, not the group that wasn't.
>
> ***Dee Speaks***

THE FINAL DRIVE

Ok, so we are now in the last month of the last quarter of the year. Our key people – our MVPs are taking the ball and running. We're letting those people run so that they can be become really well rewarded for their efforts!

I am treating them like Bill Belichick treats Tom Brady.

I am bringing them into my personal lair and putting my arm around them. We're writing plays together in the dirt and have a great camaraderie. They know they are producing their numbers. I'm telling them that when the region hits its numbers that they are going to be well compensated. They've worked really hard – them and their team, and now its reward time!

> The people that were doing well were generally very positive and upbeat when they called in.
>
> During that last month, people were very excited and couldn't wait for the celebration to start. They were always asking what was going to happen and what were we planning. The people were always trying to find out what was going on! Of course, I had to keep it top secret!
>
> You could always tell when the people that weren't doing as well called in. Those calls weren't as fun for them. Many were concerned that they were going to miss something or not be invited.
>
> But they, too, were still trying to find out what was going to happen at the celebration. Of course, they were not as positive. They wanted to know if there was something they could do to change their results... Would this work? Would that work? Would I ask Bill about this or that...? You could hear the anxiety in their voices.
>
> ***Dee Speaks***

The groups that were doing well were generally more communicative, had more ideas and their ideas were better. They were much more creative and motivated. Success breeds success. They embraced it, became a part of it, they spread their wings and wanted more.

They wanted to be a bigger part of it, more creativity and it was fun to watch. The key is to find good people and point them in the direction you want them to go. Once they take ownership, they are going to grab it and make it their own. Once they make it their own, get out of their way! They are going to make it happen and it is going to be fun.

> When people called and Bill was unavailable, they would often start talking to me about their idea. Then they would ask how I thought Bill would react or what he would say if we tried their idea?
>
> They seemed to think I knew Bill quite well. While I knew him, I didn't always know how he would respond. His perspective was much different than mine.
>
> ***Dee Speaks***

It was always interesting watching our team members interact with Dee. Many thought that if Dee liked an idea, then she might become their advocate for the idea. But Dee never took that approach. She was generally always neutral and deferred the question to me or another key staff member.

> That's true. Some felt more comfortable talking to me than others.
>
> The ones that were doing well would call more often and they liked talking to Corporate about their ideas. They seemed to brainstorm a lot more and come up with many more ideas.
>
> I think they did want to hear my opinion but also wanted to make sure Bill heard what they were saying. I would just tell them that is what I am here for, to listen.
>
> ***Dee Speaks***

In "non-business" terms, the team members took the Michigan Blizzard and went deep. The most successful and productive team members had also created team names earlier in the year. For example, their defensive line was their installers and technicians. Their offensive line included the marketing and door to door sales people. They also created tee shirts, nicknames, team names; they just took it and went very, very deep, taking the thematic process to new heights.

By the final drive, the choreography was a delight to watch. What really happened was that everyone learned how motivating it was to have fun while we were working. That enthusiasm translated into better execution and, by the end of the year, it put the entire region over the top.

The closest NFL example I can give you is that it was almost like the Steel Curtain for the Pittsburgh Steelers or the Dog Pound for the Browns. Individual teams started creating names for parts of their organization. When we saw how it was working, we grabbed it, expanded it and sent it out to all the groups. We told about how these guys are doing it and having a blast. Once others started applying the same concepts, their energy and enthusiasm increased too, as did their productivity. All of it was measurable.

Again, it was an amazing thing to watch. As the thematic process worked its way deeper and deeper into the organization, the region's productivity continued to rise. People found that they could enjoy coming to work – and that work lost its normal drudgery. Soon, I realized that the most productive groups were committed to our thematic football approach and it was not just the upper management trying to set the example.

But as this chapter title says, at this point we are in the final drive. We're still doing the Daily Call and at this point it's rah, rah and pure celebration. In many ways, I turned in to nothing more than a big cheerleader. I'm also making the rounds and doing the same thing in person.

I'm celebrating with everybody on the phone; all the while we are piling on and piling on. I'm telling them they had an awesome year and I can't wait for the big celebration that is coming.

We needed everybody's ring size so I told them to call or email Dee with their ring size. They went, "huh? Ring size, what is that all about?" Just to keep them off balance, I threw them a curve, like asking them their hat size, too. It was so much fun!

But... they don't know the details of the celebration! That's a secret – a surprise!

> Yeah, Bill would definitely tease them about the celebration.
>
> He would give them just enough information so that they would want to know more and more. I would always get calls afterwards asking what we were planning but I couldn't tell them. It was a surprise!
>
> ***Dee Speaks***

Key Take-Aways from Chapter 12

- Be a cheerleader for your team.
- Love to win – accentuate the positive.
- Recognize and celebrate activity that meets your standards.
- Make sure all of your management team is on board with you.
- Identify key players and elevate them in front of the entire organization.

Interview with Team Members

Look, this works so well that I have stolen it verbatim! The power point presentation that I start off every company with still has the original Michigan Blizzard team member's name on it from the original presentation. He's the one that put it together for the Michigan Blizzard on Bill's first presentation!

So basically for the last 10 years I have applied it to all 3 companies with tremendous success. The first time I used it was I took a position as president of a company for 4½ years. I also used it at the last two companies where I have been the CEO. Of course, we've updated, refined and nuanced for each specific situation. That said, all else is the same:

- The mission statement;
- Laying out the gameplan;
- The bias for action;
- The blocking and tackling;
- The team fundamentals;
- The team position everyone has to play; and,
- Celebrating our successes and victories!

These have all been consistent themes in every single presentation I have done: from the first company we bought in 2003 to the annual or quarterly meetings when I am in front of all of my employees. I'm always sharing our key metrics with them and sharing our successes.

We also share our failures because we want people to take risks and to occasionally fail. Like everyone, we learn more from our failures than we do our successes. We are not doing it right unless we are not afraid to try things.

Jim Holanda, CEO – RCN/Choice Cable

> I used it for 4½ years at Patriot Media from 2003 to 2007. In 2008 when we bought our Puerto Rico operation, and since NFL football carries no interest there, we changed it to a baseball theme. We've used the baseball theme ever since and have doubled our cash flow in 4 years!
>
> I know it wouldn't be a surprise to Bill, but every single one of my 1,300 employees in our current company, RCN, will proudly and gladly recite the mission statement every time I visit them. Obviously, I'm sticking with what works.
>
> **Jim Holanda, CEO – RCN/Choice Cable**

And a surprise it was!

CHAPTER THIRTEEN
CELEBRATING SUCCESS

Our Mission Statement

> ✓ *1st*
>
> ✓ *2nd*
>
> ✓ *3rd*
>
> ✓ *Celebrate Success*

At the end of a long process like this, it's easy to go in and really share your heartfelt thanks to your team.

What's important is that you have a body of work to which you can point. *It is very clear and very specific and you can say 'look at what we have achieved'!* Now it's time to celebrate!

I'm always amazed at the impact each one of us can have on another human being. Most of the time we are not even aware that the words and thoughts we convey can have such a profound effect on the other lives we touch. All too often, we simply gloss over them, but that shouldn't be the case. I have always believed that a leader's job is to manage human imagination. Help people believe in the mission and in themselves.

When you go out of your way to tell someone thank you and "great job", you should do it in a way that is heartfelt, so that it resonates and lifts people off the ground. Sometimes the effect lasts for day, while at other times it can literally last for weeks, months and even years. How many times do someone's encouraging words still resonate with us decades after they were spoken?

Here's an example:

I did a due diligence trip in Deming, New Mexico when we were looking to buy some cable properties back in 2008. During the trip I ran into the system manager in one of the cable systems I managed in the 1990's. He worked for me when I was running the west coast for Century Communications from 1995 – 1998. Somewhere in those 3 years, he did something that caught my eye. I wrote him a personal note, thanking him for his efforts, that I appreciated the great work, thanked him for being on the team and acknowledged that we were all better because of him and his efforts.

I promptly forgot about the note and went on about my business. Fast forward 10 years.

When I got out of the vehicle he comes strolling across the parking lot. He was smiling and calling to me in his wonderful way, "Mr. Bill, Mr. Bill!" He came up and gave me a big hug, asked about my family and we went to look at the plant.

After that, we went into his office building and stood by the customer care counter. While we were there, he told me that before I left he wanted to show me something. Then he went into his office and came out with a piece of paper. It was all wrinkled and it looked like somebody had occasionally been rereading it. It turned out that it was the note I wrote him 10 years ago. He kept it and it obviously meant something very special to him. I am convinced that his family had seen and read that note as well. I'm sure they all celebrated him as a father, leader and provider for their family.

Those are the kinds of things that give me goose bumps. As a leader, it's mind-boggling to think that you can have such an impact on somebody's life. As a leader, these are the kinds of things that need to be part of your repertoire.

But we need to be careful about when and how we say or write things and it always has to be from the heart. You have to be on point, talk about the specifics of what they did and how it impacted the organization. Follow that up with why you are very pleased and happy with what they did and how it helped the organization accomplish its goal.

If you just say "thanks, glad to have you on board, take care", the impact tends to have a much shorter life. Be specific and measurable with your "thank you" comments and notes, just as you are with your KPIs.

Up to now, everything we have been doing; monitoring the KPIs, the daily calls, the onsite visits, the football theme, the teams, the jerseys, the "play calling" and all the other steps we've taken have been leading up to our 'blow away the budget' accomplishments of the year.

Our efforts and accomplishments were off the charts and we set new performance and operational standards for the company. Our teams came through when we needed them and those that didn't knew that their futures lay in other occupational directions. But for those who excelled we had in store one incredible end of the year celebration!

Throughout the final quarter, preparations were underway for our end of the year extravaganza. But even before that, we kept saying that if we didn't just hit our numbers, but instead beat our numbers, we were all going to have a great time and do something none of us would ever forget.

The key message to leaders is you don't have to spend your own budget to do this. There are a lot of constituencies – vendors, suppliers, whoever provides you stuff for your company. They all have a vested interest in your success.

The first thing is to remind them what you and your organization did for them and their company. "We increased your sales by X amount, so I would like to do something great for my team. Next year we're going to do everything we can to have an even better year, which means you'll have a better year too"!

My experience is that they will sign up without question. In Michigan we got over $30,000 from vendors for our year end party. They said they wanted to be on board and they wanted to support us throughout the entire year. I never spent a dime out of my budget. Their contribution gave us the platform to do things we couldn't normally do. If you had to spend your own budget money you'd really pour over every cent. But if you have $30K to do a party for your teammates, you are going to do it right because it doesn't impact your budget. It's like found money.

Like our halftime celebration, our year end party continued the football theme. Success without a celebration can be an empty experience. Likewise, a big celebration with less than a truly dramatic success story can turn out to be a false celebration. In our case, we blew away our numbers so a really cool and dramatic celebration was an important conclusion to a heroic year.

One of the central themes of our celebration was to have a championship ring. Besides bragging rights and their bonuses, Super Bowl winners get trophies and huge, spectacular rings. We decided to do the same!

Over the course of a few months, I worked with a ring company and designed our championship ring. We did it for our Michigan Blizzard's team and we designed it in St. Louis for the Cyclone. As the design emerged, we decided on its look, the stone used in the center, its color and what writing the ring would have on the sides.

Dee sent out an email asking for the team members ring size, and she got some interesting return emails…

> Most of the responses were, "What do you want that for?"
>
> Everybody was curious and couldn't understand why we were asking for ring sizes. They would ask what kind of ring it was and I would say I don't know.
>
> I would play stupid saying, Bill didn't tell me. I would tell them that Bill was keeping it a secret, and he said we would all find out at the party.
>
> ***Dee Speaks***

So once again we started building anticipation. This is obviously happening in the 4th quarter toward the end of the year and we are not done yet. People are thinking wow, this is cool, what kind of ring, what is this going to be all about?

The other thing we did was start identifying a ton of awards. We are talking statues and trophies from 1' high to 3' high that people would have to lug home!

It is one of those things that if you think about it, most people never get trophies, except maybe when they were kids and played soccer. Everybody gets a trophy in soccer! But today most people don't have trophies sitting around in their house. If you lug this 3' trophy home, it will probably end up in a prominent place in your family room for six months or so. But after that it will be relegated to the basement bar! But that's ok – it will be a great memory and keep reminding you of what you did and how much fun you had doing it!

We gave awards for MVPs and MIPs - Most improved player! We gave awards for "offensive player of the year", "defensive player of the year" and everything we could think of from a football theme! It was a blast!

Because we were a cable company, we even received tickets for the next year's Super Bowl game from one of the sports cable programmers. That was our grand prize. The winner couldn't believe it; they actually got an all-expense paid trip to the Super Bowl How cool was that!

> The other prizes weren't anything to sneeze at either!
>
> The 2nd prize was a weekend on Michigan Avenue in Chicago with cash to spend for a really nice hotel and meals at some great restaurants and shopping.
>
> Other prizes included 4 days and 3 nights in a condo at a beach. We had large-screen TV's, jewelry, luggage, DVD's and a whole room full of prizes and stuff from Home Shopping Network, QVC, Disney, Fox and tons of trophies.
>
> ***Dee Speaks***

I actually put together a rock band, too. My Head of Engineering, John Santangelo, played guitar, my VP of Ops, Jim Holanda, was our lead guitar player, our drummer and bass player were installation technicians from one of our cable systems and I played guitar and sang lead. I rewrote the words to "Johnny Be Good" so that it was about the Charter Cyclone team. We performed it live in front of 1200 people at the America's Center (home of the St. Louis Rams). What fun!

The previous year in Michigan, the entire regional team came to the dinner in tuxedos. It was not a black tie affair for everyone else, but most everyone came in suits and long dresses. We also did a video talking about our year. We had over 1,200 partiers at both events.

The Michigan celebration was at the Grand Traverse Inn in Traverse City, Michigan. It was a huge facility and that evening the first thing I did was to do the ring ceremony. The ring winners included the management team that helped us achieve our great success.

I got up on stage and handed out the little white ring boxes to each recipient. I told everybody "do not open this - wait until everybody has their box".

I went on to tell them that what they had accomplished was an incredible feat. We started the year in chaos and, in the beginning, were a very disparate group. Some people were struggling and others didn't know which direction we were going to go. Most everyone was uncertain and a bit scared.

I told them that we went through the year and had put together an awesome team. We had our goals and objectives, we scored and we won the year. In the end, we did everything we hoped we would do. As a result of that, each person in our operation was a champion.

'Now, open your box, take out your ring and together let's put our rings on at the same time'! I told them to always remember that this is indicative of the fact that they were champions and winners and that no one could ever take that away from them.

When everyone put their rings on you could feel the goose bumps in the room. Everyone was looking at their rings and thinking, holy cow, isn't this one of the coolest things I have ever seen or ever done.

With rings on we left the room and went back to the function. I got up on stage with the senior team – in our tuxedos - and we handed out all the awards. That actually took quite some time. My senior team surprised me with an autograph book from 1967 signed by all of the Green Bay Packers including Vince Lombardi! They know just how much of a Lombardi fan I was. They also gave me a guitar signed by the Bare Naked Ladies! It was all a huge surprise!

I got a chance to talk to everyone from the corporate team on down. I spoke from the heart and told all 1,200 teammates how proud I was of each and every one of them. We also did a video that encapsulated the year 2000 and how we beat all our numbers. The video went through the cable system showing lots of our employee team members, and at the very end you could see the sun setting over a stadium and the video proclaimed "tonight when the sun sets in Michigan there is a new winning team – the Charter Michigan Blizzard"!. It was just an incredible night and one in which none of us wanted it to end.

When the video was over, there was not a dry eye in the house. That, of course, was a great time to start the party! And what a party we had! Our evening entertainment wasn't the band and me, but rather - **The Drifters**!

We danced and partied long into the night, and when it was over we all stayed right there at the Grand Traverse Lodge.

At our celebration in St. Louis, we had **The Drifters** entertain us again and we danced long into the night once again! Isn't that so much better than taking your staff to a restaurant? Which do you think they would still be talking about 10 years later?

> It was all so much fun and a night to remember!
>
> I still talk with many of the team members. We all will occasionally reminisce about how much fun it was, how we all got all dressed up and had such a great time.
>
> The management team was in tuxedos, but basically you could wear whatever you wanted. Most of the people dressed formally. The women had on long dresses and the men had suits and a lot of the people remember that and all the great prizes.
>
> The entrance was set up with balloons everywhere and it was very dramatic when you walked through. The place where we had the party was huge; there were tables everywhere, you could smell the food and everyone was really excited. You could tell when people were walking in.
>
> There were so many people coming in that it got backed up! We had over 1,200 people and had to get everyone into the room, situated, sitting down and getting them their tickets.
>
> It was pretty cool for everyone to see and as they waited their turn to come through the entrance you could feel the anticipation from everyone as the balloons guided them through the entrance into the main ballroom.
>
> ***Dee Speaks***

When I held the ring ceremony in St. Louis I did it a bit differently because it was the home of the corporate office. Unlike we did in Michigan, I held the ring ceremony in the conference room at corporate office. There, we gave out between 30 and 50 rings, which were paid for by one of our program channels. We brought everyone into that room, including Carl Vogel, then Charter's CEO who got a ring as well.

All that day I kept thinking to myself, this is a really important presentation. In Michigan, we found that this was one of those things that people really appreciate and are never going to forget. I needed to think of a way that this ring ceremony, too, would be one that would not be forgotten.

I addressed this concept in an earlier chapter but I want to highlight it again. After thinking through a few ideas, the "Evolution of Winning" flashed through my mind. I had to coin that idea – it was dead on what we experienced. So I began the ceremony by saying:

The Evolution of Winning starts with "I can't."

When I arrived here, many of you told me that "I can't do this." You tried your best and gave me lots of reasons why you couldn't do this. Then we sat down, talked things through and eventually you agreed that if we got you some training and resources, you could do this.

And you did...

The second phase of **The Evolution of Winning** *is going from "I can't" to*

"I can."

You realized that if you got the resources and support and stayed focused, that you could do that. You learned that your previous limits were just that, personal limits. That's ok, but you realized that you could only go so far with that perspective. But where the cool part comes in – I looked into everyone's eyes - and I could see their burning desire that they really wanted to be a winner and that they really wanted to do this.

And they did...

This is where the third part of **The Evolution of Winning** *kicks in – the* "**I will**" *part.*

The "I will" stage is a very special place to be. The "I will" stage is a place where only a few people get in their lives. Why? It's because most people go through the "I can't" and "I can" stage but get stuck with "I can", they never completely execute. When someone gets to the "I will" stage everyone needs to get out of the way. Why? Because that person gets so committed and so excited that they know they are going to achieve their mission. It's a take no prisoners attitude. When that happens, smart leaders just get out of the way and turn the person loose!

And they do...

The last and final stage of **The Evolution of Winning** *is what brought us here tonight: it's the* "**I did**" *stage.*

You go from "**I can't**" to "**I can**" to "**I will.**" But tonight we're here because each of you reached the "**I did**" stage. Because of that, you are all champions. You are all winners. Each of you will leave this building tonight, go home and show your family the tangible results of what you achieved. When you show your family what you've accomplished, you're going to have a large amount of pride. That's great, because you spent a lot of time and effort getting this done and achieving this goal.

And they did...

Now, everybody open up the box together and put the ring put on your finger. Let's all remember that we are winners.

Everyone on the St. Louis Central Cyclone team knew that I did a ring ceremony in Michigan and I wore my Blizzard every day to show my pride. At the St. Louis ring ceremony I wore my Michigan Blizzard ring and told them that tonight as we stand tall and we're champions I'm going to take off my Michigan Blizzard ring and from this day forward I will wear my Central Cyclone ring. I physically took of the Michigan ring and put on the Cyclone ring and I wore it every day up until I left.

The theory is if you're going to celebrate, you need to be creative and do something different that you've not done before or that your team has not seen before. Hitting your numbers and reaching your goals – **particularly when you hit or exceed your stretch goals, you have to celebrate. Otherwise, what is the point?**

After the party was over in Michigan, I was walking down the hall with Kristie. One of our Customer Service Representative's comes up to me with tears in her eyes and said, "This has made a profound change in my life and this is the coolest job I've ever had. I love this company and I never want to leave to go anywhere else." It was terribly moving for us, too.

It just shows you that *if you really do something special, really accomplish something special, you cannot let that end with a whimper. If you do, it is such a waste*. You have to put an exclamation point on it. That sets the stage for the next year and basically says that I never want to go back to the way it was. I like the way it is now and I want this to continue indefinitely.

Only then does all this become a self-fulfilling prophecy…

Key Take-Aways from Chapter 13

- Always share your heartfelt thanks with your team and individuals.
- Write encouraging words and make a difference in someone's life.
- Tap your vendors, suppliers and other parties to help you celebrate – they have a vested interest in your success too!
- Celebrate – go big or go home. Remember to make it memorable.
- Go have fun and kick some butt!!

Interviews with Team Members and Partners

> Disney was one of Charter's program suppliers, and I worked for Disney as their Vice President of National Accounts.
>
> What was unique was that Bill included us in all the meetings - even if they were operational focused. As programmers, we would provide some monetary support for his campaigns, so we were allowed to be there and listen. In the truest sense of the word, we were corporate partners within Bill's operation.
>
> We always felt that we were an integral part of what was going on. That gave me the opportunity to go to my corporate bosses at Disney and discuss how we could grow Disney's business is by supporting Bill's operation. We could do this because we were able to be part of that inner circle as to what Charter's goals and objectives were, and how as a programmer we could participate. That made a win-win.
>
> **Frank Scotello –**
> **Disney, past Vice President of National Accounts**

Interviews with Team Members and Partners

> The final celebration of the year was amazing.
>
> It was the first time I had seen an organization that, at every level – from CSR to manager – that was part of this huge celebration.
>
> It wasn't pizza for the CSRs and steak for the managers and VPs.
>
> The entire organization was there: not to some dry corporate dinner with a band later – but a huge blowout! Yes, it was incredibly fun. Everyone knew what they were celebrating and why they were there. It was truly something special for the entire regional team - and I still have my ring!
>
> Bill made me speak in front of the entire group, for which I still haven't forgiven him! I told him I don't do public speaking, and he didn't tell us until we all got there. There was that tad bit of terror that I still recall, but it was special.
>
> **Terie Hannay**
> **Past Regional Director, Customer Care, Charter Communications, Michigan**

Interviews with Team Members and Partners

> Bill had a knack for creating the finish line that everyone strove to reach. The yearend celebrations were as much about the fanfare and the recognition as it was about people just not wanting to let their team mates down and getting the rings. Not everyone has the athletic ability to reach these heights in sports; Bill makes it accessible to the athlete and the non-athlete to know what it's like to play on a championship team.
>
> **Dave Barford, past Charter Communication's COO and Senior Vice President of Charter Communication's Western Division**

> The Michigan Blizzard was a huge success that exceeded all expectations. I find several of Bill's former team mates working for us and still carrying on the same management philosophy and programs. What Bill did with the Blizzard and Cyclone teams was not just short term success, but he instilled in his people a strong propensity for extraordinary achievement. What makes business fun is watching other people become great business leaders. Bill has a legacy of coaching great managers that have gone on to create their own teams and the cycle keeps repeating itself over and over.
>
> **Dave Barford, past Charter Communication's COO and Senior Vice President of Charter Communication's Western Division**

About the Authors

Bill Shreffler is a seasoned, senior executive with 37 years of experience in the telecommunications, manufacturing, and service industries. He has started three companies, created new regions and turned poor performing operations into company leading operations on all key operating metrics. He has learned how to motivate teams, create key measurement criteria at all levels of the organization and achieve high levels of productivity and success. He is the recent past President and CEO of Pulse broadband building Fiber-To-The-Home in rural communities. Bill was also the Chairman, President and CEO of Broadstripe and President and COO of Cebridge Connections (renamed Suddenlink). He was on Charter Communication's management team as Senior Vice President of the Midwest Division serving 1.8 million customers and as Senior Vice President of two of Charter's regions. Prior to Charter Bill worked in senior management roles with several other telecommunication companies. He also has service experience with OverHead Door Company, and Hertz Corporation. Bill learned manufacturing at United States Steel and Herff Jones. He has a bachelor's degree in Accounting and a bachelor's degree in Political Science. He lives in St. Louis with his wife, son, dog, cat, two gerbils and two guinea pigs.

Jackie Smith is a former professional American football player in the National Football League. He played tight end for the St. Louis Cardinals and the Dallas Cowboys from 1963 to 1978. He has career marks of 480 receptions, 7,918 yards, and 40 touchdowns. He attended Northwestern Louisiana State University, now Northwestern State University. An outstanding football and track competitor at Northwest Louisiana, Smith joined the Cardinals in 1963. Smith was a talented receiver, a punishing blocker, a fierce competitor and an excellent runner after he caught the ball. He even handled the Cardinals' punting chores his first three seasons. Smith became the Cardinals' starting tight end during his 1963 rookie season and remained a fixture at that spot the rest of his tenure in St. Louis. The team's offensive co-captain, Smith had a string of 45 straight games from 1967 to 1970 with at least one reception. He played in 121 straight games, starting with his first NFL contest until a knee injury sidelined him in his ninth season in 1971. Injuries slowed him again in 1975 and 1976 but Smith still played in 198 games. Smith played in five straight Pro Bowls, and was named All-NFL in 1967 and 1969. He had his single-season best performance in 1967 when he had 56 receptions for 1,205 yards and nine touchdowns. After spending his entire career with the Cardinals, Smith signed with Dallas in 1978. At the time of his retirement, Smith's 7,918 receiving yards were the most ever by an NFL tight end, and would remain so until surpassed by Ozzie Newsome's 7,980 yards in 1990.

Immediately upon retirement from football, Smith became associated with Hobie Cat Boats Company of Oceanside, CA where he assists in the design and marketing of their unique fishing boats. He also spends a lot time in the boats with his 14 grandchildren in addition to attending the many sporting events they are involved in.

www.ingramcontent.com/pod-product-compliance
Lightning Source LLC
Chambersburg PA
CBHW071521180526

45171CB00002B/340